San Marino

WORLD BIBLIOGRAPHICAL SERIES

General Editors:
Robert G. Neville (Executive Editor)
John J. Horton

Robert A. Myers   Hans H. Wellisch
Ian Wallace   Ralph Lee Woodward, Jr.

John J. Horton is Deputy Librarian of the University of Bradford and was formerly Chairman of its Academic Board of Studies in Social Sciences. He has maintained a longstanding interest in the discipline of area studies and its associated bibliographical problems, with special reference to European Studies. In particular he has published in the field of Icelandic and of Yugoslav studies, including the two relevant volumes in the World Bibliographical Series.

Robert A. Myers is Associate Professor of Anthropology in the Division of Social Sciences and Director of Study Abroad Programs at Alfred University, Alfred, New York. He has studied post-colonial island nations of the Caribbean and has spent two years in Nigeria on a Fulbright Lectureship. His interests include international public health, historical anthropology and developing societies. In addition to *Amerindians of the Lesser Antilles: a bibliography* (1981), *A Resource Guide to Dominica, 1493-1986* (1987) and numerous articles, he has compiled the World Bibliographical Series volumes on *Dominica* (1987), *Nigeria* (1989) and *Ghana* (1991).

Ian Wallace is Professor of German at the University of Bath. A graduate of Oxford in French and German, he also studied in Tübingen, Heidelberg and Lausanne before taking teaching posts at universities in the USA, Scotland and England. He specializes in contemporary German affairs, especially literature and culture, on which he has published numerous articles and books. In 1979 he founded the journal *GDR Monitor*, which he continues to edit under its new title *German Monitor*.

Hans H. Wellisch is Professor emeritus at the College of Library and Information Services, University of Maryland. He was President of the American Society of Indexers and was a member of the International Federation for Documentation. He is the author of numerous articles and several books on indexing and abstracting, and has published *The Conversion of Scripts and Indexing and Abstracting: an International Bibliography*, and *Indexing from A to Z*. He also contributes frequently to *Journal of the American Society for Information Science*, *The Indexer* and other professional journals.

Ralph Lee Woodward, Jr. is Professor of History at Tulane University, New Orleans. He is the author of *Central America, a Nation Divided*, 2nd ed. (1985), as well as several monographs and more than seventy scholarly articles on modern Latin America. He has also compiled volumes in the World Bibliographical Series on *Belize* (1980), *El Salvador* (1988), *Guatemala* (Rev. Ed.) (1992) and *Nicaragua* (Rev. Ed.) (1994). Dr. Woodward edited the Central American section of the *Research Guide to Central America and the Caribbean* (1985) and is currently associate editor of Scribner's *Encyclopedia of Latin American History*.

VOLUME 188

San Marino

Adrian Edwards and Chris Michaelides

Compilers

CLIO PRESS

OXFORD, ENGLAND · SANTA BARBARA, CALIFORNIA
DENVER, COLORADO

British Library Cataloguing in Publication Data

Edwards, Adrian
San Marino. – (World bibliographical series: vol. 188)
1. San Marino – Bibliography
I. Title II. Michaelides, Chris
016.9′4549

ISBN 1–85109–242–0

ABC-CLIO Ltd.,
Old Clarendon Ironworks,
35A Great Clarendon Street,
Oxford OX2 6AT, England.

———————

ABC-CLIO Inc.,
130 Cremona Drive,
Santa Barbara,
CA 93116, USA.

Designed by Bernard Crossland.
Typeset by Columns Design and Production Services Ltd., Reading, England.
Printed and bound in Great Britain by Bookcraft (Bath) Ltd., Midsomer Norton.

THE WORLD BIBLIOGRAPHICAL SERIES

This series, which is principally designed for the English speaker, will eventually cover every country (and many of the world's principal regions), each in a separate volume comprising annotated entries on works dealing with its history, geography, economy and politics; and with its people, their culture, customs, religion and social organization. Attention will also be paid to current living conditions – housing, education, newspapers, clothing, etc.– that are all too often ignored in standard bibliographies; and to those particular aspects relevant to individual countries. Each volume seeks to achieve, by use of careful selectivity and critical assessment of the literature, an expression of the country and an appreciation of its nature and national aspirations, to guide the reader towards an understanding of its importance. The keynote of the series is to provide, in a uniform format, an interpretation of each country that will express its culture, its place in the world, and the qualities and background that make it unique. The views expressed in individual volumes, however, are not necessarily those of the publisher.

VOLUMES IN THE SERIES

Contents

Contents

Contents

Introduction

This volume is a general bibliography of books, journal articles and related material on different aspects of one of Europe's lesser-known countries, the Republic of San Marino.

San Marino

Located around Mount Titano's triple limestone peaks in the Apennine Mountains, San Marino is a so-called micro-state. It covers just 61.196 square kilometres (24.1 square miles), and is entirely surrounded by Italy. San Marino is both the name of the republic and the name of its small capital city located at the top of the mountain.

Tradition states that in 301 AD a group of Christians led by Marinus, a stone-mason from Rab (Arbe) in Dalmatia, arrived on the mountain looking for refuge. There they built a religious community around a small church, and, as the name of Saint Marinus spread, others crossed the Adriatic Sea to join them. In time, a monastery was established and a town grew up at its gates; documentary evidence states that there were already towers and strong defensive walls by the year 951.

Both the monastery and the commune appear to have prospered and retained their independence, staying outside the control of local bishops. San Marino's territory grew and by the thirteenth century it was approximately the size it is now, with its own statutes and a system of government based on consuls, the precursors of today's Captains Regent.

Relations were uneasy with the neighbouring Papal States throughout the following centuries. Indeed, the entire population was excommunicated by Pope Innocent IV during the 1240s. Whilst the two states were officially at war during the fourteenth and fifteenth centuries, other forces sought the opportunity to assert their influence. Chief among these were the Malatesta family of Ravenna, but it was the Dukes of Urbino who gained the upper hand by offering their protection, eventually signing a treaty with San Marino in 1549.

Urbino's influence did not last long, and the tiny republic managed to maintain its independence when much of surrounding Italy came under the influence of Venice, the Papal States, or later Spain and Austria: 1739 saw the last time that San Marino was occupied by a foreign force. The Legate for Romagna, Cardinal Giulio Alberoni, frustrated that the Papal States had failed to incorporate the Republic into its territories, took it upon himself to lead a small army across the borders and seize control. Appeals to the Pope by the people of San Marino resulted in Enrico Enriquez, the Governor of Perugia, being sent to mediate. He judged that Alberoni had exceeded his powers and on 5 February 1740 the occupying troops were ordered to leave.

When Napoleon invaded Italy in 1797, he sent a messenger to San Marino's government stating that it was his duty to preserve the country's independence as an example of freedom. This independence was further recognized internationally at the 1815 Congress of Vienna.

The Republic effectively remained neutral throughout the Risorgimento, offering refuge to several Italian nationalists. The most significant of these was Giuseppe Garibaldi, who was forced to flee Rome in 1849 when French forces came to the aid of the Pope. At the end of the political upheavals in 1862, the newly formed Kingdom of Italy formally recognized San Marino.

The twentieth century has seen the Republic remain neutral during both World Wars (although sixty-three people were accidentally killed by British bombs in 1944). In the political arena, a Fascist government was in power from 1923 until a communist–socialist administration took over at the end of the Second World War. For twelve years, San Marino was the only country in Western Europe to be run by a communist government. A coalition of Christian Democrats (Partito Democratico Cristiano Sammarinese) and the Socialist Party (Partito Socialista Sammarinese) currently forms the government, having most recently been returned to power in May 1993.

Today, San Marino maintains its independence whilst being part of the wider Italian-speaking cultural area of southern Europe. It is a member of the United Nations, the Council of Europe, the Conference on Security and Cooperation in Europe, and has signed various treaties with the European Union. Its currency is the Italian lira, although it mints its own coins. The country's population is 24,399 (1994), with a further 11,000 living abroad. Most people live in the towns, in either Serravalle–Dogana in the north within easy reach of Rimini, or near the top of Mount Titano in Borgo Maggiore and the city of San Marino itself. The other major settlements are Acquaviva, Cailungo, Chiesanuova, Domagnano, Faetano, Falciano, Fiorentino,

Gualdicciolo, Montegiardino, Murata and Ventoso. The population is very homogeneous, being entirely Italian-speaking (the older population still using a local dialect analogous with that of the neighbouring region of Emilia-Romagna) and almost completely Roman Catholic. There are no ethnic minorities, but there are large numbers of Italian residents.

San Marino's constitution has fascinated observers for centuries. There are two heads of state at any one time, the Captains Regent (Capitani Reggenti), who hold power together for six-monthly periods but who cannot be re-elected for three years. These figure-heads continue the tradition of the two consuls first recorded in the thirteenth century. Legislative power is held by the sixty-member Great and General Council (Consiglio Grande e Generale), which is elected every five years by universal suffrage. Legal matters are decided by the Council of the Twelve (Consiglio dei XII), and there is a Congress of State (Congresso di Stato) – consisting of three secretaries of state and seven ministers – which exercises executive power. The Republic has its own legal system, police force and civil defence corps. For local administration, the country is divided into nine *castelli* (former parishes), each with its own elected council.

The economy is dominated by tourism; around three million visit the country each year, the largest part of these being Italian day-trippers. Other sources of revenue include exports of textiles, tiles and ceramics, furniture, chemicals, wine and postage stamps. Unlike the Vatican City, the other micro-state surrounded by Italy, San Marino contains arable land, where wheat, barley, maize and vines are cultivated. There is no stock exchange.

The country has comprehensive social programmes and the state endeavours to find employment for all. Welfare programmes include income support schemes, generous state pensions, and free medical provision. Education is also free and is compulsory from six to fourteen years of age. There is a school of music (Istituto Musicale), and a university (Università degli Studi della Repubblica di San Marino), with departments of history, semiotics, technology, bio-medicine, education and law.

Because of its small size, small population and dependence on Italy, San Marino lacks some of the institutions normally encountered in a sovereign state. For example, telephone services are provided by SIP, the Italian national telecommunications company. The country's two home-grown daily newspapers are only a couple of years old, these being *Il Quotidiano Sammarinese* and *Il Corriere di San Marino*. There is, however, a local television station (San Marino RTV) and an independent radio station (Radio Titano), but the famous 'San Marino

Grand Prix' in Formula One motor racing is held over the border at Imola, and the San Marino national soccer team usually plays its major international fixtures in Bologna. Anyone strolling around the little capital city will also note a lack of foreign embassies; only Italy, the Holy See and the Sovereign Military Order of Malta have embassies there.

Besides its own coins, used side-by-side with those minted by the Italian government, San Marino has produced its own postage stamps since 1877; these are popular among collectors, especially in Italy.

A brief note on terminology. The official name of the country is 'The Republic of San Marino' (La Repubblica di San Marino), and it is under this name that the country currently signs its treaties with other nations. However, an alternative – more ceremonial form – is also encountered, this being 'The Most Serene Republic of San Marino' (La Serenissima Repubblica di San Marino). The associated adjective in Italian is the slightly irregular 'sammarinese' (plural: 'sammarinesi'), for which there is no consistently used English form, although the compilers of this volume have favoured 'Sanmarinese'.

About the bibliography

The aim of this annotated, general bibliography is to act as an introduction on all aspects of San Marino for the researcher, librarian, student, traveller and general reader.

There was great interest in San Marino during the late nineteenth century. Many writers in the English-speaking world were intrigued by the way in which it had escaped becoming part of a unified Italy. Interest appears to have waned during the twentieth century. Indeed, San Marino does not feature in many of the standard reference tools found on library shelves in English-speaking countries. For example, there is no entry in *Commercial laws of the world* or *International tax treaties of all nations*. Even in Italian there is no encyclopaedia of San Marino, no national atlas and no national biography. Considerable gaps in the coverage given by general monographs and journal articles can be identified in areas such as the social sciences. Within the borders of San Marino itself, the range of published material is fairly small; at the time of writing there were in fact only two commercial book publishers, and any country with such a small population is statistically unlikely to produce many writers or artists. In the past, those that there were often moved to Italy and were assimilated into the Italian cultural tradition.

The bibliography itself is arranged into subject chapters, the arrangement of which follows that of other volumes in this series but is significantly influenced by the nature of the material available. Entries within the chapters have been organized alphabetically by title. The chapters are preceded by a chronology of significant dates in the country's history and a list of Captains Regent who have held office during the twentieth century. Authors, titles and subjects (including people and places) are indexed at the end of volume, where there is also a map showing the location of the principal settlements; whilst researching the bibliography, the compilers discovered that such maps are quite difficult to come by.

Although there has been a concerted effort to identify English-language material, often the definitive or only material on a subject is in Italian. Given that many general readers might not speak Italian, references to material in French and German have also been included. In all cases where the item is not in English, a translation of the title has been supplied.

Sources

The largest part of the items listed in this bibliography can be found in the British Library. However, a variety of other libraries were consulted, not least the British Architectural Library at the Royal Institute of British Architects, the Italian Institute and a variety of public reference libraries.

Acknowledgements

The compilers are pleased to acknowledge the help of colleagues in the various departments and reading rooms of the British Library, both in London and Yorkshire, of Elisabetta Righi Iwanejko, director of the Biblioteca di Stato di San Marino, and of Cristina Mularoni of the Republic's Dipartimento Affari Istituzionali.

Finally, we should like to point out that the compilation of this bibliography has proved to be a rewarding project, and the compilers hope that scholars, librarians, travellers and the general reader will find it interesting and useful.

Useful Addresses

Ufficio di Stato per il Turismo (State Office for Tourism)
Palazzo del Turismo
Contrada Omagnano, 20
47031 San Marino Città
Republic of San Marino
tel. (+378) 882410
fax. (+378) 990388

Biblioteca di Stato (State Library)
Palazzo Valloni
Contrada Omerelli, 13
47031 San Marino Città
Republic of San Marino
tel. (+378) 882248
fax. (+378) 882295

Biblioteca Universitaria (University Library)
Università degli Studi della Repubblica di San Marino
Contrada delle Mura, 16
47031 San Marino Città
Republic of San Marino
tel. (+378) 882500
fax. (+378) 882303

Musei di Stato (State Museums)
c/o Galleria Nazionale d'Arte Moderna
Scala Bonetti, 2
47031 San Marino Città
Republic of San Marino
tel. (+378) 882670
fax. (+378) 882679

Museo Postale Filatelico e Numismatico (Philatelic and Numismatic Museum)
Piazza Grande, 24
47031 Borgo Maggiore
Republic of San Marino
tel. (+378) 903958

Centro di Studi Storici Sammarinesi (Centre for Historical Studies on San Marino)
Contrada San Francesco, 4
47031 San Marino Città
Republic of San Marino
tel. (+378) 882513

Centro Elaborazioni Dati e Statistica (Centre for Statistics and Data Processing)
Viale Antonio Onofri, 109
47031 San Marino Città
Republic of San Marino
tel. (+378) 885125
fax. (+378) 885127

Chronology

3rd century   According to legend, Marinus and Leo, stonecutters from Arbe (on the Dalmatian coast) come to Rimini, following Emperor Diocletian's edict to rebuild the town, which had been destroyed by Demosthenes, King of the Liburnians.

Marinus spends twelve years at Rimini. He takes refuge in the caves of Baldaserrona to escape from a woman who claims to be his wife and eventually moves to the top of Mount Titano where he lives as a hermit and builds the monastery of St Peter.

4th century
301   Traditionally the foundation date of the Republic.

366   *3 September* Presumed date of death of Saint Marinus.

6th century
511   Earliest documentary mention of Mount Titano by name in a letter by the monk Eugippio indicating the existence of a monastery.

8th century
754   Act of donation of lands to Pope Stephen II by Pepin the Short, King of the Franks. These include the 'Castellum Sancti Marini', proof of the co-existence of a secular community with the religious one.

9th century
885   The *Placito Feretrano* records the decision of a tribunal to award certain lands to Stephen, Abbot

of the Monastery of San Marino, against the claims of Delto, Bishop of Rimini.

10th century
951

The *Diploma di Berengario,* which states that San Marino had already constructed its towers and city walls, establishes the existence of a 'plebs', the embryo of the twelfth-century commune.

13th century
1244

Documents show that a system of government is in operation, with two Consuls holding power. The territory has by now increased from four to twenty-six square kilometres. Compulsory military service has been introduced.

1247-49

All San Marino citizens excommunicated by Pope Innocent IV.

1253

The Arengo, the council of heads of families, delegates its powers to a council composed of a smaller number of people.

1291

A priest named Teodorico is unsuccessfully sent to persuade the Sanmarinese to become subjects of the Pope.

1295-1302

San Marino's earliest set of Statutes.

14th century
1320

Peace is signed after decades of conflict between San Marino and the encroaching bishops of Montefeltro.

1371

Cardinal Anglico, General Vicar of the Holy See, includes San Marino in the vicariate of Montefeltro. The Commune retains, however, a degree of autonomy, having its own Statutes and Heads of State.

15th century
1437

The Castle of Serravalle is given its own statutes by Sigismondo Pandolfo Malatesta, Lord of Rimini.

1440-42   San Marino is involved in the wars between the Montefeltros and the Malatestas.

1448   First description of San Marino as a Republic.

1463   After the defeat of Sigismondo Pandolfo Malatesta by Federico II da Montefeltro, Duke of Urbino, the territories of Fiorentino, Faetano, Montegiardino and Serravalle are given to San Marino, the Duke's ally.

16th century
1503   Cesare Borgia, son of Pope Alexander IV, invades San Marino in an attempt to create a principality between Romagna and the Marches. His plans are thwarted by the death of Alexander IV later in the year. All occupied territories are returned to their former owners.

1507   Death of Guidobaldo, the last of the Montefeltro rulers. The Duchy of Urbino is now ruled by the Della Rovere family.

1543-49   Neighbouring states unsuccessfully attempt to invade the Republic.

1549   Defence treaty signed with Guidobaldo II, Duke of Urbino.

1550-60   Internal power struggles between the Brancuti and Belluzzi families for the control of the Republic. Order is re-established through the intervention of Guidobaldo II, Duke of Urbino.

1566   Guidobaldo II is named First Councillor of the Republic.

17th century
1600   New statutes approved by the Great and General Council establish the economic and political power of the Sanmarinese oligarchy.

1602   The Republic signs a treaty of protection with Pope Clement VIII.

1609
Completion of the Convent of St Clare, the building of which had started some forty-four years earlier.

1631
After the death without an heir of Francesco Maria II della Rovere, the Duchy of Urbino is absorbed into the Holy See and San Marino is for the first time surrounded by a single, powerful state. The Republic's autonomy is, however, guaranteed by the treaty of 1602.

18th century
1737-38
Marino Belzoppi, Marino Ceccoli and Pietro Lolli (a former Captain Regent) conspire to overthrow the Government and to assassinate its representatives. Their attempt fails. Lolli's family appeals to the Cardinal Giulio Alberoni, Legate for Romagna. The Cardinal's offer to mediate is rejected by the San Marino Government.

1739
Cardinal Alberoni tries to incorporate San Marino into the Papal States and occupies the Republic with a small army. Appeals to the Pope result in Enrico Enriquez, Governor of Perugia, being sent to mediate. He decides that the cardinal had exceeded his powers.

1740
5 February Alberoni's forces leave.

1785-86
Civil and social unrest led by Tommaso Rinaldini della Isabellona ('Mason dla Blona'), a bandit and popular hero.

1796
23 June Concerned about Napoleon's Italian Campaign, the San Marino Government issues an edict outlawing all refugees to the Republic

1797
5-7 February Napoleon requests the surrender of Monsignor Ferretti, Bishop of Rimini who has taken refuge in the Republic, taking with him ecclesiastical treasures. The Government is prepared to comply with the request but Ferretti manages to escape, leaving behind his treasures which are handed to the French.

8-12 February Gaspar Monge visits the Captains Regent bringing a message of friendship and peace from Napoleon and proposing the expansion of San Marino to the Rimini coast. The offer is rejected in order to maintain the Republic's autonomy.

3 June A petition is presented to the Government demanding the abolition of the nobility.

25 June Establishment of a Committee of Public Safety whose aim is to suppress revolt.

1798   Thanks to the diplomatic skills of Antonio Onofri San Marino establishes friendly relations with the Cisalpine Republic and the Roman Republic.

1799   Melchiorre Delfico, philosopher, statesman and future historian of San Marino, finds refuge in the Republic.

19th century
1802   San Marino signs a treaty with Napoleon's Italian Republic.

1815   San Marino's independence is internationally recognized at the Congress of Vienna.

1814-61   San Marino acts as a refuge for many Italian nationalists, including Garibaldi in 1849.

1817   First convention with the Holy See concerning the import of salt and tobacco.

1821   Bartolomeo Borghesi is given refuge in San Marino. He will take an active part in the political life of the Republic and become a focus for the Risorgimento.

1824   Death of Pope Pius IV who is succeeded by Leo XII. Relations between San Marino and the Holy See deteriorate because the Republic offers shelter to political exiles. In the following years the Holy See will make various demands for their extradition.

1825	*25 February* Death of Antonio Onofri.
1825-38	Construction of a neoclassical basilica to replace the former parish church.
1833	The first post office opens in San Marino.
1846	San Marino allows Vatican troops to enter its territory and arrest political refugees.
1849	After the fall of the Roman Republic Garibaldi, pursued by the Austrians, seeks refuge in San Marino. Domenico Maria Belzoppi, one of the Captains Regent, attempts to dissuade him in order to avoid compromising the neutrality of the Republic. Garibaldi, nevertheless, enters San Marino with 1,500 soldiers and 300 horses. The Government attempts to mediate but Garibaldi rejects the conditions suggested and escapes with 150 men. Austrian troops enter San Marino and seize whatever arms of the Garibaldini they can find.
1851	San Marino is surrounded by Austrian troops trying to capture exiles who have taken refuge in the Republic.
1853	Assassination of Gian Battista Bonelli, Secretary of State.
1855	Cholera epidemic.
1858	Opening of the State Library.
1862	The new Kingdom of Italy signs an agreement recognizing the sovereignty of San Marino.
1864	San Marino coinage minted for the first time.
1865	First official census of the population of San Marino. First postal convention between Italy and San Marino.

1876	Foundation of the Società Unione e Mutuo Soccorso (Unity and Mutual Aid Society).
1877	San Marino issues its first postage stamp and signs a postal agreement with Italy.
1879	Giuseppe Angeli sets up the first printing press in San Marino and will go on to publish newspapers opposed to the oligarchic government of the Republic. These will include *Il Giovane Titano* (1881), *La Lotta* (1883), and *Il Radicale* (1889).
1881	Foundation of the Cassa di Risparmio di San Marino (San Marino Savings Bank).
1894	Inauguration of the Palazzo del Governo.
1899	Inauguration of the State Museum.

20th century
1900	Workers protest against the Government.
1902-6	Political campaign for the return of sovereignty to the Arengo, with the newspaper *Il Titano* (1903) as its mouthpiece.
1902	The first issue of the Catholic periodical *Il Giovane Montefeltro* is published in San Marino.
1906	*25 March* A referendum removes power from the Consiglio Principe e Sovrano (Chief and Sovereign Council) and returns it to the Arengo.
	June First elections for representatives to the Council; victory of the progressive democratic groups over the conservatives.
	24 July The name of the Council is changed to Consiglio Grande e Generale (Great and General Council).
1909	Establishment of the Unione Cattolica Sammarinese (San Marino Catholic Union). Its official organ is the newspaper *Sammarino*.

Support for the Catholic movement will be stronger in the countryside whereas the socialists will be in control of urban centres.

1914   Foundation of the Società Operaia di Mutuo Soccorso (Workers' Mutual Aid Society). Its aim is to assist workers in the country, thus complementing the work of the Società Unione e Mutuo Soccorso (Unity and Mutual Aid Society) whose influence is stronger in urban centres.

1922   Foundation of the Fascist Party of San Marino.

1925-43   Gino Zani undertakes an extensive restoration programme of San Marino's public buildings, churches and fortifications.

1926   The Fascists gain overall control of the Government.

1927   A convention is signed with Italy for the construction of a railway line from Rimini to San Marino. The line will be inaugurated in 1932.

1932   Publication of *La Voce del Titano*, a semi-clandestine newspaper printed by dissident Fascists, denounces the Government's abuse of power.

1933   Failed coup attempt against the Fascist Government.

1939   Convention of Friendship and Good Neighbourliness signed with Mussolini's government, establishing a customs union and total currency and monetary integration between the two countries and forming the basis for subsequent treaties.

1941   Foundation of the San Marino Communist Party, which is to remain illegal until 1945.

1943   *28 July* Three days after the fall of the Fascist régime in Italy anti-Fascist demonstrators in San

Marino form a 'Comitato della Libertà' which establishes a provisional government.

5 September The democratic and anti-Fascist parties win the general elections.

28 October The Council delegates its powers to a Council of State which includes citizens of different ideological persuasions. It is led by Ezio Balducci and its remit is to maintain the Republic's neutrality.

1944   The Republic offers hospitality to refugees after the bombing of Rimini at the end of 1943. By August their numbers exceed 100,000.

26 June The British accidentally bomb the Republic, killing sixty-three people.

20 November After the defeat of the Germans at Valdragone, the Allied Forces enter San Marino City. Allied troops will remain stationed there for two months.

1945   The ten-person Congress of State founded to govern the country on a day-to-day basis.

1955   The Communist party comes to power.

1956   Opening of the Premio d'Arte Figurativa del Titano, the first major exhibition organized in San Marino. It includes 1,500 works by 515 artists and attracts some 100,000 visitors. In 1959 the exhibition will change its name to Biennale d'Arte and will become international in scope. There will be four more biennial exhibitions which will include retrospectives of the work of major contemporary artists.

1957   An alternative provisional Government is set up at Rovereta.

1960   Women are given the right to vote.

1972   San Marino starts minting its own coinage again after a gap of some thirty years.

1973	Women are given the right to hold high office.
1979	Foundation of a 'Consulta' to represent the interests of Sanmarinese communities abroad.
1983	The State Library and the State Museum become separate organizations.
1992	Customs agreement with European Union comes into force.

Captains Regent of San Marino

San Marino has two heads of state at any one time, the Captains Regent (Capitani Reggenti). They act jointly, with a reciprocal right of veto. They are appointed by the Great and General Council and they serve for a period of six months, with investitures taking place in April and October. This means that in any year, four people will have served as head of state. A citizen may hold the post of Captain Regent many times, but has to wait three years before being able to stand again.

Captains Regent, 1900-95

1900	1. Domenico Fattori/Antonio Righi
	2. Giovanni Bonelli/Pietro Ugolini
1901	1. Luigi Tonnini/Marino Nicolini
	2. Antonio Belluzzi/Pasquale Busignani
1902	1. Onofrio Fattori/Egidio Ceccoli
	2. Gemino Gozi/Giacomo Marcucci
1903	1. Federico Gozi/Nullo Balducci
	2. Marino Borbiconi/Francesco Marcucci
1904	1. Menetto Bonelli/Vincenzo Mularoni
	2. Luigi Tonnini/Gustavo Babboni
1905	1. Antonio Belluzzi/Pasquale Busignani
	2. Onofrio Fattori/Piermatteo Carattoni
1906	1. Giovanni Belluzzi/Pietro Francini
	2. Alfredo Reffi/Giovanni Arzilli
1907	1. Ciro Belluzzi/Francesco Pasquali
	2. Giuseppe Angeli/Francesco Valli
1908	1. Menetto Bonelli/Gustavo Babboni
	2. Olinto Amati/Raffaele Michetti
1909	1. Luigi Tonnini/Domenico Suzzi-Valli
	2. Marino Borbiconi/Giacomo Marcucci

1910	1. Alfredo Reffi/Giovanni Arzilli
	2. Giovanni Belluzzi/Luigi Lonfernini
1911	1. Moro Morri/Cesare Stacchini
	2. Onofrio Fattori/Angelo Manzoni-Borghesi
1912	1. Gustavo Babboni/Francesco Pasquali
	2. Menetto Bonelli/Vincenzo Marcucci
1913	1. Giuseppe Angeli/Ignazio Grazia
	2. Ciro Belluzzi/Domenico Suzzi-Valli
1914	1. Domenico Fattori/Ferruccio Martelli
	2. Olinto Amati/Cesare Stacchini
1915	1. Moro Morri/Antonio Burgagni
	2. Alfredo Reffi/Luigi Lonfernini
1916	1. Onofrio Fattori/Ciro Francini
	2. Gustavo Babboni/Giovanni Arzilli
1917	1. Egisto Morri/Vincenzo Marcucci
	2. Angelo Manzoni Borghesi/Giuseppe Balducci
1918	1. Ferruccio Martelli/Ermenegildo Mularoni
	2. Protogene Belloni/Francesco Morri
1919	1. Dominico Vicini/Pietro Suzzi-Valli
	2. Moro Morri/Francesco Pasquali
1920	1. Marino Rossi/Ciro Francini
	2. Carlo Balsimelli/Simone Michelotti
1921	1. Marino della Balda/Vincenzo Francini
	2. Egisto Morri/Giuseppe Lanci
1922	1. Eugenio Reffi/Giuseppe Arzilli
	2. Onofrio Fattori/Giuseppe Balducci
1923	1. Giuliano Gozi/Filippo Mularoni
	2. Marino Borbiconi/Mario Michetti
1924	1. Angelo Borghesi/Francesco Mularoni
	2. Francesco Morri/Girolamo Gozi
1925	1. Marino Fattori/Augusto Mularoni
	2. Valerio Pasquali/Marco Marcucci
1926	1. Manlio Gozi/Giuseppe Mularoni
	2. Giuliano Gozi/Ruggero Morri
1927	1. Gino Gozi/Marino Morri
	2. Marino Rossi/Nelson Burgagni
1928	1. Domenico Suzzi-Valli/Francesco Pasquali
	2. Francesco Morri/Melchiorre Filippi
1929	1. Girolamo Gozi/Filippo Mularoni
	2. Ezio Balducci/Aldo Busignani
1930	1. Manlio Gozi/Marino Lonfernini
	2. Valerio Pasquali/Gino Ceccoli

1931	1. Angelo Borghesi/Francesco Mularoni
	2. Domenico Suzzi-Valli/Marino Rossi
1932	1. Giuliano Gozi/Pompeo Righi
	2. Gino Gozi/Ruggero Morri
1933	1. Francesco Morri/Settimio Belluzzi
	2. Carlo Balsimelli/Melchiorre Filippi
1934	1. Marino Rossi/Giovanni Lonfernini
	2. Angelo Borghesi/Marino Michelotti
1935	1. Federico Gozi/Salvatore Foschi
	2. Pompeo Righi/Marino Morri
1936	1. Gino Gozi/Ruggero Morri
	2. Francesco Morri/Gino Geccoli
1937	1. Gino Gozi/Settimo Belluzzi
	2. Marino Rossi/Giovanni Lonfernini
1938	1. Manlio Gozi/Luigi Mularoni
	2. Carlo Balsimelli/Celio Gozi
1939	1. Pompeo Righi/Marino Morri
	2. Marino Michelotti/Orlando Reffi
1940	1. Angelo Borghesi/Filippo Mularoni
	2. Federico Gozi/Salvatore Foschi
1941	1. Gino Gozi/Secondo Menicucci
	2. Giuliano Gozi/Giovanni Lonfernini
1942	1. Settimio Belluzzi/Celio Gozi
	2. Carlo Balsimelli/Renato Martelli
1943	1. Marino Michelotti/Bartolomeo Borghesi
	2. Marino Della Balda/Sante Lonfernini
1944	1. Francesco Balsimelli/Sanzio Valentini
	2. Teodoro Lonfernini/Leonido Suzzi-Valli
1945	1. Alvaro Casali/Vittorio Valentini
	2. Feruccio Martelli/Secondo Fiorini
1946	1. Giuseppe Forcellini/Vincenzo Pedini
	2. Filippo Martelli/Luigi Montironi
1947	1. Marino Della Balda/Luigi Zafferani
	2. Domenico Forcellini/Mariano Ceccoli
1948	1. Arnaldo Para/Giuseppe Renzi
	2. Giordano Giacomini/Domenico Tomassoni
1949	1. Feruccio Martelli/Primo Bugli
	2. Vincenzo Pedini/Agostino Biordi
1950	1. Giuseppe Forcellini/Primo Taddei
	2. Marino Della Balda/Luigi Montironi
1951	1. Alvaro Casali/Romolo Giacomini
	2. Domenico Forcellini/Giovanni Terenzi

1952	1. Domenico Morganti/Mariano Ceccoli
	2. Arnaldo Para/Eugenio Bernardini
1953	1. Vincenzo Pedini/Alberto Reffi
	2. Giordano Giacomini/Giuseppe Renzi
1954	1. Giuseppe Forcellini/Secondo Fiorini
	2. Agostino Giacomini/Luigi Montironi
1955	1. Domenico Forcellini/Vittorio Meloni
	2. Primo Bugli/Giuseppe Maiani
1956	1. Mario Nanni/Enrico Andreoli
	2. Mariano Ceccoli/Eugenio Bernardini
1957	1. Giordano Giacomini/Primo Marani
	2. Marino Franciosi/Federico Micheloni
1958	1. Zaccaria Savoretti/Stelio Montironi
	2. Domenico Forcellini/Pietro Reffi
1959	1. Marino Belluzzi/Agostino Biordi
	2. Giuseppe Forcellini/Feruccio Piva
1960	1. Alvaro Casali/Gino Vannucci
	2. Eugenio Reffi/Pietro Gianecchi
1961	1. Federico Micheloni/Giancarlo Ghironzi
	2. G. Vito Marcucci/Pio Galassi
1962	1. Domenico Forcellini/Francesco Valli
	2. Antonio Morganti/Agostino Biordi
1963	1. Leonido Suzzi-Valli/Stelio Montironi
	2. Giovan Franciosi/Domenico Bollini
1964	1. Marino Belluzzi/Eusebio Reffi
	2. Giuseppe Micheloni/Pier Mularoni
1965	1. Ferruccio Piva/Federico Carattoni
	2. Alvaro Casali/Pietro Reffi
1966	1. Francesco Valli/Emilio Della Balda
	2. G. Vito Marcucci/Francesco Francini
1967	1. Vittorio Rossini/Alberto Lonfernini
	2. Domenico Forcellini/Romano Michelotti
1968	1. M. Benedetto Belluzzi/Dante Rossi
	2. Pietro Giancecchi/Aldo Zavoli
1969	1. Ferruccio Piva/Stelio Montironi
	2. Alvaro Casali/Giancarlo Ghironzi
1970	1. Francesco Valli/Eusebio Reffi
	2. Giuseppe Lonfernini/Simone Rossini
1971	1. Luigi Lonfernini/Attilio Montanari
	2. Federico Carattoni/Marino Vagnetti
1972	1. M. Benedetto Belluzzi/Giuseppe Micheloni
	2. Rosolino Martelli/Bruno Casali

1973	1. Francesco Francini/Primo Bugli
	2. Antonio Volpinari/Giovan Franciosi
1974	1. Ferruccio Piva/Giordano Reffi
	2. Francesco Valli/Enrico Andreoli
1975	1. Alberto Cecchetti/Michele Righi
	2. Giovannito Marcucci/Giuseppe Della Balda
1976	1. Primo Bugli/Virgilio Cardelli
	2. Clelio Galassi/Marino Venturini
1977	1. Alberto Lonfernini/Antonio Volpinari
	2. Tito Masi/Giordano Reffi
1978	1. Francesco Valli/Enrico Andreoli
	2. Ermenegildo Gasperoni/Adriano Reffi
1979	1. Marino Bollini/Lino Celli
	2. Giuseppe Amici/Germano De Biagi
1980	1. Pietro Chiaruzzi/Primo Marani
	2. Giancarlo Berardi/Rossano Zalferani
1981	1. Maria Pedini-Angelini/Gastone Pasolini
	2. Mario Rossi/Ubaldo Biordi
1982	1. Giuseppe Maiani/MArino Venturini
	2. Libero Barulli/Maurizio Gobbi
1983	1. Adriano Reffi/Massimo Rossini
	2. Germano De Biagi/Renzo Renzi
1984	1. Giorgio Crescentini/Gloriana Ranocchini
	2. Marino Bollini/Giuseppe Amici
1985	1. Enzo Colombini/Severino Tura
	2. Pier Paolo Gasperoni/Ubaldo Biordi
1986	1. Marino Venturini/Ariosto Maiani
	2. Giuseppe Arzilli/Maurizio Tomassoni
1987	1. Renzo Renzi/Carlo Franciosi
	2. Gian Franco Terenzi/Rossano Zafferani
1988	1. Umberto Barulli/Rosolino Martelli
	2. Luciano Cardelli/Reves Salvatori
1989	1. Mauro Fiorini/Marino Vagnetti
	2. Leo Achilli/Gloriana Ranocchini
1990	1. Adalmiro Bartolini/Ottaviano Rossi
	2. Cesare A. Gasperoni/Roberto Bucci
1991	1. Domenico Bernardini/Claudio Podeschi
	2. Edda Ceccoli/Marino Riccardi
1992	1. Germano De Biagi/Ernesto Benedettini
	2. Romeo Morri/Marino Zanotti
1993	1. Patricia Busignani/Salvatore Tonelli
	2. Gian Luigi Berti/Paride Andreoli

Captains Regent of San Marino

1994	1. Alberto Cecchetti/Fausto Mularoni
	2. Renzo Ghiotti/Luciano Ciavatta
1995	1. Marino Bollini/Settimio Lonfernini
	2. Piero Natalino Mularoni/Marino Venturini

The Country and Its People

1 **Dall'alto del Titano.** (From the top of Titano.)
  Carlo Sgarbi. Lugo, Italy: Walberti, 1992. 222p.

The author, a historian of San Marino, devotes eighteen short chapters to various aspects of the history and culture of the Republic. These include reminiscences about notable Sanmarinese such as Giuseppe Mastella, the poet and Greek scholar; Pietro Franciosi, the socialist thinker and historian; Ezio Balducci, the noted doctor; and Carlo Delcroix, the Second World War hero.

2 **A freak of freedom, or, The Republic of San Marino.**
  J. Theodore Bent. Bologna, Italy: Analisi Trend, 1985. 271p.
  (Biblioteca Storica della Repubblica di San Marino).

This is a facsimile reproduction of J. T. Bent's work originally published in London in 1879 by Longmans, Green & Co. The author spent much time in San Marino, eventually becoming an honorary citizen, but was disappointed that there was so little reliable material written about the Republic. This work combines a detailed history with a contemporary description of the country and its institutions. It includes an interesting comparison of San Marino with Switzerland, the Hanseatic League towns and Andorra. The volume contains illustrations based on the author's own sketches.

3 **Let's visit San Marino.**
  Noel Carrick. Basingstoke, England: Macmillan, 1988. 95p. map.
  (Let's Visit series).

Though primarily intended for young readers, this is a useful general survey of the Republic and its people. It includes sections on the history, government, culture, economy, social life and customs, stamps and coins of San Marino.

4 **The little five.**
Sam Waagenaar. London: André Deutsch, 1960. 72, 96p.
(Zwarte Beertjes, no. 157-8).
The brief text in this multilingual work on Europe's small states precedes a collection of black-and-white photographs, showing life in the late 1950s. The 'little five' of the title are San Marino, Andorra, Liechtenstein, Monaco and the Vatican City.

5 **A minute in the life of San Marino.**
Bruce McCall. *The New Yorker*, vol. 64 (20 June 1988), p. 27.
A witty account of how a group of internationally known photographers documented a minute in the life of the Republic.

6 **Our littlest ally.**
Alice Rohe. *National Geographic Magazine*, vol. 34 (Aug. 1918),
p. 139-63.
This is a thorough, affectionate and faintly patronizing portrait of San Marino and its people, with sections about the country's history, government, economy and customs. It is also significant as a historical document with its description of social conditions in the Republic on the morrow of the First World War (e.g. a Sanmarinese baby christened not after the Republic's patron saint but after President Wilson). It is accompanied by seventeen excellent black-and-white photographs taken by the author.

7 **The state orders of the Republic of San Marino.**
Vincent Powell-Smith. *The Armorial*, vol. 3, no. 2 (May 1992),
p. 112-14.
A concise essay on the state orders given by the Republic, these being Orders of Merit, the Equestrian Order, the Order of Saint Agatha and various types of awards for chivalry. The medals and insignia are described in detail but not illustrated.

8 **Storia, araldica e diritto nobiliare nella Serenissima Repubblica di San Marino.** (History, heraldry and noble right in the Most Serene Republic of San Marino.)
Arnolfo Cesari D'Ardea. *Hidalguía*, year 35, no. 200 (Jan.-Feb. 1987),
p. 17-30.
This Italian-language article in a Spanish journal begins with a brief introduction to the Republic's history and goes on to consider the development of the role of the Captains Regent. The coats-of-arms of the Republic and its 'castelli' (local authorities) are described, but not illustrated and the heraldic orders listed. Finally, there is a paragraph on each of the forces of law and order.

9 **Studi Sammarinesi: Scienze, Arte e Lettere.** (Sanmarinese Studies: Science, Arts and Literature.)
San Marino: Società di Studi Sammarinesi, 1984- . annual. bibliogs.
This annual periodical contains Italian-language material on a wide range of subjects. Each volume contains scholarly articles relating to San Marino, followed by collections of poetry and short stories.

10 **Terra di San Marino: leggende e storia.** (Land of San Marino: legends
and history.)
Edited by Manlio Gozi. Milan, Italy: Bolla, 1934. new ed. 494p.

Although dating from the interwar years, this work probably remains the most
comprehensive work devoted entirely to San Marino, its people and their culture. It
consists of about 150 items, including essays and poems, covering most aspects of
life, from early history to festivals, military history to visual arts and literature. The
work contains forty-eight photographs showing the Republic during the early years of
this century. The author was one of the key players in Sanmarinese politics during the
Fascist period.

11 **Les trois petites républiques: Saint-Marin, Andorre, Moresnet.**
(The three little republics: San Marino, Andorra, Moresnet.)
Léon Jaybert. Paris: C. H. Durandin, 1873. 75p.

Pages 1-16 are devoted to San Marino, tracing its legend and discussing its
government and constitution. It also offers some general information about the
country.

Geography

General

12 **Il territorio.** (The land.)
Conrad Mularoni. In: *Storia illustrata della Repubblica di San Marino.* San Marino: AIEP, 1985, p. 17-32. maps. bibliog.

A general survey of the physical geography of San Marino, looking at geological characteristics, lithology, morphology and geodynamic evolution, with a brief section on fossils. The article contains several geological maps and photographs.

La trasformazione del territorio. (The transformation of the land.)
See item no. 201.

Geology

13 **Contributo alla conoscenza della geologia di San Marino.**
(Contribution to the study of the geology of San Marino.)
Giuliano Ruggieri. *Giornale Geologico* (Bologna), vol. 25 (1953), p. 49-80. map.

Ruggieri gives an overview of the geology of the Republic, describing it as a series of Miocene outliers on clay formations. Similarities are pointed out between the calcareous clays found in San Marino and those found in parts of Algeria.

14 **Geologia di S. Marino.** (Geology of San Marino.)
Giuliano Ruggieri. *Studi Romagnoli*, vol. 9 (1958), p. 3-9. maps.
bibliog.

This article, based on a conference paper read at the 1957 conference of the Society of
Romagnol Studies, contains the results of the writer's geological investigations carried
out in the years 1953-57. The work identifies the rock and soil types found in the
Republic, with the conclusions shown in diagrammatic form.

15 **Il Monte Titano, territorio della Repubblica di San Marino: i suoi
fossili, la sua età ed il suo modo d'origine.** (Mount Titano, territory of
the Republic of San Marino: its fossils, its age and its origin.)
A. Manzoni. *Bollettino del Real Comitato Geografico d'Italia*, no. 1-2
(Jan.-Feb. 1873), p. 3-28; no. 3-4 (March-April 1873), p. 67-84.

This article looks at the geological aspects of Mount Titano, the rock on which the city
of San Marino is built. It looks in detail at the fossil evidence, giving tables which
classify finds made to date, including large numbers of *Sphaerodus cinctus*, *Bryozoi*
and *Nummulites planulata*. In the second part of the article, the writer attempts a
chronology of the mountain's formation, based on this and other evidence. The work
is well supported by bibliographical references.

Cave e scalpellini: dall'epoca di Marino al XIX secolo. (Caves and
stonecutters: from the time of Saint Marinus to the nineteenth century.)
See item no. 142.

Maps

16 **San Marino.**
Bologna, Italy: Studio F. M. B., 1982. 1 folded map. (Piante di Città.
Conosci il Mondo, no. 133).

This 80 × 100 cm colour street plan of the entire republic is on a scale of 1:12,000.
All streets and country roads are named, and the borders between the *castelli* (local
administrative areas) are shown. There are more detailed inset plans at a scale of
1:4,000 of the city of San Marino with Borgo Maggiore, Serravalle, Montegiardino
and Dogana. Both the main map and the insets show the location of schools, churches,
cemeteries and other public amenities; the more detailed plans show a selection of
places of interest. The reverse includes a few notes about the country and an
alphabetical index to street names.

Tourism

17 **Europe's micro-states.**
P. Jenner, C. Smith. *International Tourism Reports*, no. 1 (1993),
p. 68-89.

According to this article, Andorra, Liechtenstein, Monaco and San Marino all receive large numbers of day trippers, but have difficulty in enticing visitors to stay overnight (San Marino has just 50,000 overnight visitors a year). Only Andorra has any degree of success, due largely to its ski resorts. This article takes a look at the tourist industry in each of the four countries and considers its impact on their economies.

18 **Turismo e vie di comunicazione.** (Tourism and means of
communication.)
M. Antonietta Bonelli. In: *Storia illustrata della Repubblica di San
Marino*. San Marino: AIEP, 1985, p. 477-92. bibliog.

Bonelli looks at the history of the two interrelated subjects of transportation infrastructure and tourism. The article begins by looking at roads both within San Marino and those linking the Republic with Rimini, with an especially large amount of information on the situation around the year 1800. Other topics studied include the Rimini–San Marino railway, and bus and helicopter services. The author then goes on to look at the Sanmarinese 'vocation' for tourism and the reasons why it came late to the Republic. Key events in the development of the industry are considered, including the introduction of mains water and electricity, the opening of the new government building in 1894, the abolition of passport controls with Italy, the inclusion of San Marino in travel guides, and the importance of the railway. Much statistical information is given, and the article contains several photographs and a special bibliography on the Rimini–San Marino railway line.

Travel

Travel guides

19 **Emilia Romagna.**
Marco Ancarani. Verona, Italy: Edizioni Futuro, 1988. 222p. maps.
This guide to the Italian cultural region of Emilia-Romagna includes a section devoted to San Marino (p. 116-21). The principal monuments are described and there are lists of hotels and restaurants. Other useful addresses are given and suggestions are made about souvenir buying.

20 **Guida di San Marino.** (Guide to San Marino.)
M. V. Brugnoli, E. Zocca. Rome: Libreria dello Stato, 1953. 68p. map.
This is primarily a guide to the city of San Marino, concentrating on describing the main buildings, monuments and fortifications. Additionally there are photographs of many of the works of art to be found in the city's museums, supported by an index of artists.

21 **Guide to the Republic of San Marino.**
C. Neville Packett. Bradford, England: The author, [1965?]. 48p. map.
An English-language typescript guide book to San Marino, containing a general history of the Republic and a description of the principal monuments and buildings of the capital, with a brief mention of those in Borgo Maggiore, Serravalle, Montegiardino and Dogana.

22 **Italia: guida illustrata.** (Italy: an illustrated guide.)
Milan, Italy: Touring Club Italiano. 528p. maps.
The section on San Marino (p. 415) is a useful quick-reference source for the traveller.

23 **San Marino: ancient land of liberty.**
Bologna, Italy: Italcards, 1988. 2nd ed. 117p. maps.

This English edition of an Italian tourist guide contains a large number of photographs, a detailed map of the city of San Marino, and entries on most of the historic monuments and other sights of interest, including the Philatelic Museum in Borgo Maggiore.

24 **Umbria, the Marches and San Marino.**
Christopher Catling. London: A.& C. Black, 1994. 185p. map.
(Black's Italian Regional Guides).

Chapter fourteen (p. 173-8) is dedicated to San Marino. There is practical information for the traveller, a short historical outline and a description of the old town.

Travellers' accounts

25 **From Rome to San Marino: a walk in the steps of Garibaldi.**
Oliver Knox. London: Collins, 1982. 204p. map. bibliog.

Garibaldi was forced to flee Rome in 1849, marching across central Italy to San Marino. This is the diary of Oliver Knox as he retraces the route of this Retreat from Rome, in the spring of 1980.

26 **The little tour.**
Giles Playfair, Constantine FitzGibbon. London: Cassell, 1954. 222p. maps. bibliog.

In 1953, Playfair, accompanied by his 'collaborator' FitzGibbon, travelled to Andorra, Liechtenstein, Monaco and San Marino. He spent three months in San Marino, and the account of his time there (p. 163-210) is witty yet full of historical information. The text is accompanied by eight contemporary photographs.

27 **The smallest republic in the world: a visit to San Marino.**
W. Miller. *The Westminster Review*, vol. 144, no. 3 (1895), p. 284-93.

The first part of this article is an account of a trip made to San Marino by the writer in the 1890s, with a description of how the city then looked. The second part consists of an outline of the Republic's history, its government and the main state institutions.

28 **Viaggiatori e stranieri a San Marino**. (Travellers and visitors in San Marino.)
M. Antonietta Bonelli. In: *Storia illustrata della Repubblica di San Marino*. San Marino: AIEP, 1985, p. 461-76.

Although San Marino appears infrequently on the itineraries of travellers to the Italian peninsula it has, nevertheless, fascinated historians, men of letters and statesmen on account of its history and its ability to maintain its freedom over the centuries, running counter to the general pattern of historical development. This article examines the development of the image of San Marino as a geographical, historical and political entity in the descriptions of writers, especially American and French ones, from the sixteenth to the nineteenth century. American views include that of the diplomat George Washington Erving who visited San Marino in 1812-13 and considered the Republic to be one of the six wonders that justified a journey to the peninsula (the other five being Venice, the antiquities of Rome, Pompeii, Herculaneum and Paestum). San Marino was also praised by John Adams and Abraham Lincoln, the latter stating that, though its territory was small, the Republic was one of the most honourable in history. French views include that of George Sand, who compared the Republic to Andorra and praised its tradition of offering refuge to the persecuted, and of Montesquieu who visited San Marino and somewhat deflated the legend that its perpetual freedom was related to the wisdom and virtue of its people by saying that the only reason the Republic had managed to survive was because it was not really worth bothering about.

29 **Una visita alla Repubblica di S. Marino.** (A visit to the Republic of San Marino.)
Carlo Scarabelli. In: *Poveri bimbi!: una visita alla Repubblica di S. Marino.* Grosseto, Italy: F. Perozzo, 1876, p. 53-110.

A description of the author's visit to San Marino in 1871. It is full of facts, including an example of the state budget, and is interspersed with historical vignettes.

Flora and Fauna

General

30 **Guida alla natura d'Italia.** (Guide to nature in Italy.)
Gianni Farneti, Fulco Pratesi, Franco Tassi.   Milan, Italy: Mondadori,
1984. 4th ed. 570p.

Arranged by region and habitat, this work is a guide to the flora and fauna found on
the Italian peninsula. The section on mountain habitats in Emilia-Romagna (p. 200-4),
contains drawings of the kind of wildlife seen in the San Marino area.

Flora

31 **Field guide to the wild flowers of southern Europe.**
Paul Davies, Bob Gibbons.   Marlborough, England: Crowood Press,
1993. 320p.

Despite its title, this pocket guide actually covers most kinds of flora, including trees
and bushes. Its geographical coverage extends from Iberia, through southern France
and Italy south of the Alps, to Malta. It, therefore, includes the wild plantlife found in
San Marino. The work contains descriptions of about 1,200 species, most of which are
illustrated with colour photographs. The narrative gives details about geographical
distribution, habitat and flowering times, but does not include indigenous names.
There is a glossary of botanical terms based on line-drawings.

32 **La flora: lineamenti della vegetazione della Repubblica di San Marino.** (Flora: an outline of the vegetation of the Republic of San Marino.)
Andrea Suzzi Valli. In: *Storia illustrata della Repubblica di San Marino.* San Marino: AIEP, 1985, p. 1-16. map. bibliog.

This article looks at vegetation in San Marino by habitat type, such as downy oak woodland, meadow, and white willow and poplar scrub, with the species found in each habitat type being described in detail. The piece is illustrated with a number of photographs and drawings. There is also a Latin-to-Italian list of some 140 plants mentioned in the text, and a vegetation map of the Republic.

33 **Flora d'Italia.** (Flora of Italy.)
Sandro Pignatti. Bologna, Italy: Edagricole, 1982. 3 vols. bibliog.

The geographical area covered by this reference work extends beyond Italy to Corsica, Malta, southern Switzerland, the Julian Alps of Slovenia, Istria in Croatia and San Marino. There are several informative essays at the beginning of volume one, including a history of botanical studies in Italy. The main part of the work is arranged by orders, families and species in line with *Flora Europaea*. Physical descriptions in Italian are accompanied by line-drawings and outline maps indicating main areas of distribution. Latin, Italian and dialectal names are given. The work is well indexed.

34 **Flora italica.**
Pietro Zàngheri. Padua, Italy: CEDAM, 1976. 2 vols. bibliog.

This two-volume work is a reference guide to flora that is either indigenous, naturalized or widely cultivated in Italy and the surrounding areas. Both pteridophytes and spermatophytes are included. The work is arranged by classes of flora, then by orders and families. The written description for each is in Italian, and contains details of the plant's height, distribution (San Marino falls within Emilia in this case), subspecies, whether it is annual, biannual or perennial, and the months in which it flowers. Latin names are used for the arrangement of entries, but Italian names are also given; there are indexes in both languages. The first volume contains text, the second plates of line-drawings.

35 **Generalità sullo studio fitosociologico della vegetazione boschiva nella Repubblica di San Marino.** (General remarks on the phytosociological study of woodland vegetation in the Republic of San Marino.)
Andrea Suzzi Valli. *Studi Sammarinesi*, vol. 1 (1984), p. 185-92.

Nowhere in San Marino is far from human habitation, and as a result woodland and scrub now account for just 8.1 per cent of landcover. However, ruderal-nitrophilous plant habitats are on the increase, especially at higher altitudes. This article analyses the content of the sub-Mediterranean deciduous woodland vegetation centred around *Quercetalia pubescentis*, describing the varieties typically found there.

Fauna

36 **La fauna.** (Fauna.)
Andrea Suzzi Valli, Viero Amadei.   In: *Storia illustrata della*
Repubblica di San Marino.   San Marino: AIEP, 1985, p. 653-68.

The fauna of San Marino is that of the Apennines of the Emilia-Romagna and the
Marches. This article gives brief descriptions of the most representative animals of the
territory, both vertebrate and invertebrate. It includes twenty-four colour illustrations
and also a list of 127 species of birds present in San Marino, indicating their rarity and
territoriality.

37 **Fauna d'Italia.** (Fauna of Italy.)
Bologna, Italy: Calderini, 1956- . bibliogs.

This is an irregular scientific periodical published under the aegis of the Italian
National Academy of Entomology and the Zoological Union of Italy, with support
from the Italian Ministry of the Environment. Issues are monographic in nature, each
looking at a different order or family of fauna found in Italy and surrounding areas. To
date around thirty have been published, all in Italian, with illustrations and
bibliographies.

38 **Gli uccelli d'Italia.** (The birds of Italy.)
Giacinto Martorelli.   Milan, Italy: Rizzoli, 1960. 3rd ed., revised by
Eduardo Moltoni. 859p.

This is possibly the major reference work on bird life in Italy, and therefore includes
those species seen in San Marino. The volume is arranged according to order of
species and then family. The entries discuss the geographical distribution of each
species, its physical characteristics and life-cycle. Drawings and photographs
accompany the text. Species names are given in Italian and Latin only.

Prehistory, Archaeology and Palaeontology

39 **Paleontologia sammarinese.** (The palaeontology of San Marino.)
Conrad Mularoni. *Studi Sammarinesi*, vol. 1 (1984), p. 129-45.

The rocks of San Marino have proved to be rich in fossils, many of which are on display in museums in Bologna and Florence. This article consists primarily of a catalogue of finds. Entries are arranged according to the geology in which the fossils were discovered, and then by zoological class (foraminifers, corals, echinoids, etc.). The article contains four photographs.

40 **La preistoria sammarinese.** (Sanmarinese prehistory.)
Onofrio Fattori. *Libertas Perpetua: Museum*, year 4, no. 1 (Oct. 1935-April 1936), p. 188-202.

Written by the then curator of the National Museum, this article concentrates on archaeological finds made principally from 1850 to 1911. Artefacts discovered include Bronze Age axe-blades and razors.

41 **L'uomo e il Titano: i primi insediamenti.** (Man and Titano: the first settlements.)
Dario Giorgetti. In: *Storia illustrata della Repubblica di San Marino.* San Marino: AIEP, 1985, p. 33-60. bibliog.

This article is in two parts. The first looks at pre-Bronze Age San Marino, beginning with its geological formation and discussing the evidence for Neolithic settlement in the area; it includes brief sections on the origins of man and on Pebble Culture. The second part considers human habitation in the Republic from the Bronze Age to the dawn of Roman civilization. Both parts contain drawings and photographs of finds from San Marino and neighbouring parts of Italy.

La cultura materiale: agricoltura ed archeologia rurale. (Material culture: agriculture and rural archaeology.)
See item no. 152.

History

General

42 **Come se non fosse nel mondo: la Repubblica di San Marino dal mito alla storia.** (As if not of this world: the Republic of San Marino from myth to history.)
Rodolfo Montuoro. San Marino: Edizioni del Titano, 1992. 141p. bibliog. (La Città Felice).

This work considers the connections between myth and history. It looks at the concept of San Marino and all it stands for from earliest times through to the end of the last century and the socialist thinker and politician Pietro Franciosi. Large numbers of references to San Marino in historical documents are tracked down and discussed.

43 **Discorso pronunciato nell'aula del Pubblico Palazzo per l'ingresso degli eccellentissimi Capitani Reggenti Libero Barulli I, Maurizio Gobbi I.** (Speech made in the hall of the Palazzo Pubblico on the entrance of their excellencies the Captains Regent Libero Barulli I and Maurizio Gobbi I.)
Denis Mack Smith. San Marino: [n.p.], 1982. 14p.

The Speech surveys the Republic's ability to resist external aggression and retain its independence through the ages; it also includes some useful references to English writers on San Marino, notably Joseph Addison whose views on the constitution of the country influenced, among others, John Adams who is said to have used it as a model for the constitution of the United States.

44 **Guida storica-artistica illustrata della Repubblica di San Marino.**
(Illustrated historical and artistic guide to the Republic of San Marino.)
Francesco Balsimelli. San Marino: The Government, 1932. 3rd ed.
228p.

Balsimelli's historical introduction to San Marino lays emphasis on describing the country's institutions. Portraits of the main personalities of the 1930s are included. There is also a list of the works of art to be found in the Pinacoteca dello Stato.

45 **La libertà perpetua di San Marino.** (The continual freedom of San
Marino.)
Giosuè Carducci. Bologna, Italy: Zanichelli, 1947. 54p.

A transcript of the speech made by the influential Italian poet Giosuè Carducci in 1894 on the occasion of the opening of the Palazzo degli Offici (later Palazzo Pubblico or Palazzo del Governo). It considers the history of Sanmarinese independence and is accompanied by bibliographical references and photographs.

46 **Libro d'oro della Repubblica di San Marino.** (Social register of the
Republic of San Marino.)
Marchese de Liveri di Valdausa. Foligno, Italy: Feliciano Campitelli,
1914. 278p. map.

This major work on the history of the Republic contains a large number of illustrations, principally photographs of buildings and portraits of notable citizens from the late nineteenth and early twentieth centuries. In addition, there are extensive lists of officials from earliest times, including Captains Regent and law commissioners, with biographical information in some cases. Recipients of State honours are also recorded.

47 **Lungo cammino di un popolo sulla strada della libertà.** (The long
path of a people on the road to freedom.)
Alvaro Casali. Urbania, Italy: Bramante, 1970. 230p.

Casali's work is principally a general introductory history to San Marino, arranged in short chapters with photographs and the texts of important documents. To a lesser extent it looks at the culture of the country, with several poems about the Republic being included.

48 **Relazione della Repubblica di San Marino, La Repubblica di San
Marino.** (Report on the Republic of San Marino, The Republic of San
Marino.)
Pietro Ellero, Giovanni Battista Fascioli. Bologna, Italy: Li Causi,
1984. 90, 71p.

This volume contains two works in facsimile, first published in 1868 and 1875. Both give detailed histories of the Republic from its inception until the date of writing, with a strong emphasis on the constitution.

49 **Ricordi storici della Repubblica di San Marino.** (Historical notes on the Republic of San Marino.)
Marino Fattori. Florence, Italy: Felice Le Monnier, 1956. 8th ed. by Onofrio Fattori. 121p. bibliog.

A history of the Republic from 301 AD to the Second World War, organized into sixty-seven short chapters. It includes some post-war photographs of the capital. Marino Fattori was the major nineteenth-century San Marino historian; this edition has been updated by his son, Onofrio Fattori.

50 **San Marino: mito e storiografia tra i libertini e il Carducci.**
(San Marino: myth and historiography from the Libertines to Carducci.)
Aldo Garosci. Milan, Italy: Edizioni di Comunità, 1967. 396p.
(Cultura e Realtà, no. 76).

Much of San Marino's history, both ancient and modern, is surrounded by myth. In this work, the author attempts to look at both the facts and the fiction of various events and periods of the country's past, linking this with the Sanmarinese need to establish a sense of identity. The work contains a large number of bibliographical references.

Early and medieval

51 **L'Alto Medioevo: il *Placito Feretrano*.** (The early Middle Ages: the *Placito Feretrano*.)
Carlo Dolcini. In: *Storia illustrata della Repubblica di San Marino.*
San Marino: AIEP, 1985, p. 61-76.

The *Placito Feretrano* is a fundamental text for the history of Romagna, Montefeltro and, more especially, San Marino because it establishes the existence in 885 AD of a monastery in San Marino and its territory, and its rivalry with the Bishop of Rimini. It records a court decision taken in that year recognizing certain lands as the possessions of the monastery against the claims of Delto, the Bishop of Rimini, who failed to prove that his Church had ever been in possession of these lands. The document was discovered by Annibale degli Abati Olivieri in 1749 but it was not until 1957 that an accurate reading of the text was established by Cesare Maranesi who also indicated that the surviving text is that of an eleventh-century copy. The authenticity of the document has been questioned by various scholars. As well as examining these claims the article also looks at legal documents, dated 1069 and 1070, which record the Bishop of Rimini's donation of the lands mentioned in the *Placito* to the monastery of San Gregorio in Conca. The author's conclusion is that part of the text of the *Placito* may be an eleventh-century interpolation.

52 **Il comune.** (The commune.)
   Carlo Dolcini. In: *Storia illustrata della Repubblica di San Marino.*
   San Marino: AIEP, 1985, p. 93-108. bibliog.

Focusing primarily on documentary evidence, this article looks at the development of the commune of San Marino during the medieval period. The text begins with Cardinal Anglico's description of the lands and laws of the castle of San Marino in his *Descriptio Romandiole* of 1371, and then steps back to consider the factors that influenced the development of this fiercely independent commune. Topics considered include the importance of relations with the Bishops of Montefeltro and the various statutes of 1295-1302, 1317 and 1352-53. The text is accompanied by several reproductions of documents held in the State Archive.

53 **L'economia rurale in un comune malatestiano: gli Statuti di
   Serravalle del 1437.** (Rural economy in a commune of the Malatesta:
   the Serravalle Statutes of 1437.)
   Laura Rossi, Pier Paolo Guardigli. In: *Le Signorie dei Malatesti: atti
   [di] una giornata di studi malatestiani a San Marino.* Rimini, Italy:
   Bruno Ghigi, 1990, p. 39-53. (Atti delle Giornate di Studi Malatestiani,
   no. 18).

In 1437 Sigismondo Pandolfo Malatesta permitted the Castle of Serravalle to have its own Statutes, partly in recognition of its strategic importance. They were composed in vernacular Italian and were contained in four books: civil procedures, penal procedures, 'estraordinarii' measures and 'danni dati'. The Statutes remained in force even after Serravalle's incorporation into the commune of San Marino as part of the latter's commitment to continuing the Castle's autonomy. The author of this paper, presented at a conference of Malatesta studies, laments that the Statutes have been so little studied to date. After establishing the historical context, he shows how much they reveal about everyday rural life in the lands governed by the Castle of Serravalle.

54 **Fatti e momenti di vita comunale.** (Facts and episodes from life in the
   commune.)
   Cristoforo Buscarini. *Studi Sammarinesi*, vol. 5 (1988), p. 67-103.

This article consists of a collection of studies by Buscarini on fourteenth- and fifteenth-century documents. In the first, he studies various official papers from Cardinal Anglic Grimoard de Grisac, Vicar Apostolic and Legate of Romagna 1368-72. Most of these have been examined many times before, but Buscarini identifies a few that have been largely overlooked, and which shed light on the subject of San Marino and its autonomy from the Catholic Church. This piece is continued in later issues of *Studi Sammarinesi*. The second looks at documents relating to San Marino's involvement in the war between the Papacy and the Malatesta family in the 1460s, and includes a transcript of a letter sent by Bartolo di Francesco di Pilo to the Captains of San Marino. The third piece traces the life of Roberto Malatesta through documents held by the Archivio di Stato, whilst the final essay looks at the last years of Federico Malatesta, and is followed by transcripts of contemporary documents.

55 **La leggenda 'Sancti Marini': una storia religiosa tra Rimini
e il Monte Titano.** (The legend 'Sancti Marini': a religious story from
Rimini and Mount Titano.)
Riccardo Burigana. San Marino: AIEP, 1992. 137p. bibliog.

In this examination of the legend of Saint Marinus, the author attempts to learn
something of religious life around Mount Titano from when it was first Christianized
in the third century AD up until the ninth century. The first part of the work is a
transcription of the manuscript *Vita Sancti Marini* held in the National Library of
Turin (ms. F III 16), with variants from other works recorded as footnotes. No
translation of the Latin original is given. The second part consists of a detailed
commentary working through the text section by section, discussing what is happening
and identifying what it tells us about the historical context. The volume contains
indexes of personal and place names, an index to biblical references, and a
bibliography.

56 **Notizie di Roberto Malatesti e della 'Guerra di Rimini' dalle carte
sammarinesi.** (Notes from Sanmarinese documents on Roberto
Malatesta and the 'War of Rimini'.)
Cristoforo Buscarini. In: *Le Signorie dei Malatesti: atti [di] una
giornata di studi malatestiani a San Marino.* Rimini, Italy: Bruno
Ghigi, 1990, p. 99-108. (Atti delle Giornate di Studi Malatestiani,
no. 18).

The writer of this conference paper laments that manuscripts held by the San Marino
State Archives have generally been ignored by Italian scholars of Montefeltro and
Rimini history. In order to promote them, he describes in general terms the content of
some of the more important documents from the fifteenth to the seventeenth century,
particularly those that shed light on Roberto Malatesta and on events of the 1460s.
Many of the papers discussed were sent to the Captains Regent by Roberto Malatesta
himself. The paper contains no extracts or photographs of the documents.

57 **La Repubblica di San Marino durante l'esilio dell'Alighieri.**
(The Republic of San Marino during the exile of Dante Alighieri.)
Giuseppe Pochettino. *Studi Sammarinesi*, vol. 6 (1989),
p. 131-43.

Although not published until 1989, this piece is in fact the text of a speech made by
Pochettino on 1 April 1907. He begins by wondering why Dante never made any
reference to San Marino in his work, despite his interest in 'liberty'. The main part of
the text is concerned with describing historical events, politics and society in the early
part of the fourteenth century, the time when Dante was in exile from Florence. This is
followed by an assessment of how much he might have known about San Marino, the
author disputing the view that Dante may have visited nearby S. Leo in 1307. There is
an interesting if flowery section on what San Marino represented in the eyes of the
Italians at the beginning of the twentieth century.

58 **Il Santo Marino.** (Saint Marinus.)
Carlo Dolcini. In: *Storia illustrata della Repubblica di San Marino.*
San Marino: AIEP, 1985, p. 77-92. bibliog.

This work gives a summary of the legend of Saint Marinus, the Dalmatian stonecutter who sought peace and refuge on Mount Titano. His life is described in a number of manuscripts, the earliest of which dates from the tenth century. Legend has it that he lived in the fourth century but the author surveys recent scholarship and concludes that the sixth or seventh century is a more likely supposition. The controversy regarding the present location of the Saint's relics (it has been suggested that they are not in the Basilica of San Marino but that they were translated to Lombardy in Longobard times) is also examined. The article includes a list of all extant manuscripts of the *Vita Sancti Marini* and a bibliography and is profusely illustrated with colour plates of works depicting the Saint.

59 **Signorie e principati.** (Signories and principalities.)
Laura Rossi. In: *Storia illustrata della Repubblica di San Marino.*
San Marino: AIEP, 1985, p. 125-40. bibliog.

Rossi gives an account of San Marino's policies from the fourteenth century, when the Republic depended on the diocese of Montefeltro, to 1631, when the death of Francesco Maria della Rovere I, who died without a successor, meant that with the absorption of the duchy of Urbino into the Papal States, San Marino was surrounded, for the first time, by a single powerful and extensive state. During this period the Republic's external policies were guided by the need to safeguard its autonomy. In the fifteenth century its alliance with the Montefeltros against the Malatestas brought to it, in the 1463 treaty, the castles of the latter, nearly doubling its territory. The article also examines political, institutional, economic and administrative changes in the Republic. Its relative isolation meant that its cultural achievements during the Renaissance were limited. The contribution of some notable Sanmarinese jurists (Marino Calcigni, Costantino Bonelli, Giuliano Corbelli) and artists (Antonio Orafo, Giovan Battista Belluzzi) is examined. The activities of these men were largely outside San Marino; they often travelled widely and worked in various cultural centres in Italy.

60 **Il territorio ed il castello di San Marino attraverso i secoli.**
(The territory and castle of San Marino through the centuries.)
Gino Zani. Faenza, Italy: Fratelli Lega, 1963. 183p. maps.

This is a substantial work containing a large number of photographs of the city and detailed maps of showing the growth of the Republic. The text deals mainly with the period from the ninth to the fifteenth centuries, and the last chapter looks at the construction and history of the castle.

La Repubblica di San Marino e gli statuti del 1352-53. (The Republic of San Marino and the statutes of 1352-53.)
See item no. 123.

Modern (1463-)

61 **31 agosto e non 31 luglio: breve storia di una cerimonia e della sua contesta preparazione.** (31 August and not 31 July: a short history of a ceremony and its disputed preparation.)
Maria Antonietta Bonelli. *Studi Sammarinesi*, vol. 1 (1984), p. 15-23.

The author of this article claims that San Marino's monument to Garibaldi was not inaugurated on 31 July 1882 as generally believed, but on 31 August 1882. Using contemporary published and manuscript material, the article describes the political controversy that the monument caused and explains why neither of the Captains Regent was present at its unveiling.

62 **Antifascisti emiliani e romagnoli in Spagna e nella Resistenza.**
(Emilian and Romagnolo anti-Fascists in Spain and the Resistance.)
Luigi Arbizzani. Milan, Italy: Vangelista, 1980. 237p. (Storia del Mondo Contemporaneo).

Many San Marino citizens volunteered to join Italians from Emilia-Romagna in the fight against Fascism during the Spanish Civil War of the 1930s. Later they were involved in the Italian resistance against Mussolini. This work identifies who they were and documents the part they played.

63 **Antonio Onofri.**
Marco Pelliconi. In: *Storia illustrata della Repubblica di San Marino*.
San Marino: AIEP, 1985, p. 285-300. bibliog.

Onofri (1759-1825) was the leading statesman of his time, being Captain Regent seven times between 1791 and 1821. This article looks at his life and contribution to Sanmarinese politics, government and diplomacy, including his role during the crisis of 1797 when it looked possible that Napoleon would invade the Republic. It also considers the significant part Onofri played in the political life of the country and his involvement in establishing relations with the newly re-created Church States after the 1815 Congress of Vienna. The text is accompanied by several reproductions of portraits and poems dedicated to Onofri, and a document written by him recounting a meeting he had with Napoleon in June 1805.

64 **Le bande garibaldiane a San Marino.** (Garibaldi fighters in San Marino.)
Oreste Brizi. Arezzo, Italy: Filippo Borghini, 1850. 58p.

Throughout the Risorgimento, San Marino officially stood to one side, resisting the temptation to join the growing demands for Italian unity. In 1849 it gave refuge to Giuseppe Garibaldi, the Italian nationalist, whilst he was being pursued by Austrian and Papal troops. This work is a straightforward historical account of these events.

65 **Bonaparte, le Premier Empire et la République de Saint-Marin.**
(Bonaparte, the First Empire and the Republic of San Marino.)
André Lorion. *Revue de l'Institut Napoléon*, vol. 135 (1979), p. 39-44.
Throughout the Napoleonic period in Italy, San Marino retained its independence.
This article describes the negotiations that took place from 1797 to 1814 between
France, its client states and the Sanmarinese government, as a feature of the
republican sympathies of the Napoleonic regime.

66 **Briganti a San Marino.** (Bandits in San Marino.)
Alfio Cavoli. In: *Storia illustrata della Repubblica di San Marino*.
San Marino: AIEP, 1985, p. 253-68. bibliog.
In the eighteenth century there were various outbursts of criminal activity against the
corrupt oligarchical government of the Republic. In 1737 Marino Belzoppi and Pietro
Lolli conspired to overthrow the government and assassinate its representatives. The
article also gives an account of the activities of Sebastiano Bora (called 'Puiena')
whose band terrorized Montefeltro, but it concentrates on the story of Tommaso
Rinaldini della Isabellona (called 'Mason dla Blona'), one of the most remarkable
instances of civil and social rebellion in the Romagna and the Marches region.
Rinaldini, who became something of a popular hero, managed, between 1785 and
1786, repeatedly to escape arrest and humiliate the specially enlisted papal guard.

67 **Il cardinale Alberoni e la Repubblica di San Marino: studi e
ricerche.** (Cardinal Alberoni and the Republic of San Marino: studies
and research.)
Carlo Malagola. Bologna, Italy: Zanichelli, 1886. 752p.
The first part of this work describes the event in 1739 when Cardinal Giulio Alberoni,
the Papal Legate for the Province of Romagna, tried to incorporate San Marino into
the Papal States. Initial attempts to convince Pope Clement XII that the Sanmarinese
people wanted to abandon their independence failed, and so Alberoni invaded the
Republic with a small army. Much of the capital was looted, and the Pope sent an
envoy to examine the situation. It was declared that Alberoni had exceeded his
authority, and his forces were ordered to leave. The second part of the work consists
of transcriptions of 160 documents, principally the correspondence between the
different parties.

68 **Garibaldi e la Repubblica di San Marino.** (Garibaldi and the Republic
of San Marino.)
Pietro Franciosi. Florence, Italy: Sansoni, 1949. 64p.
This work, originally published in 1891, looks at the links between the Italian
nationalist Giuseppe Garibaldi and San Marino. After fleeing Rome in 1849, Garibaldi
marched across central Italy to San Marino, where he sought refuge from Austrian and
Papal troops. This story is recounted in detail and supported by transcriptions of
various documents, including letters between Garibaldi and the Captains Regent.

69 **Il mito di San Marino: immagini del mito e tracciati di storia tra XVII e XIX secolo.** (The myth of San Marino: images of the myth and historical sketches from the seventeenth to the nineteenth centuries.) Rodolfo Montuoro. In: *Storia illustrata della Repubblica di San Marino.* San Marino: AIEP, 1985, p. 334-48. bibliog.

In the seventeenth and eighteenth centuries San Marino was seen as a model state and was compared to the Greek city states and the Italian medieval republics. It was admired for its ability to maintain its freedom over centuries of political turmoil and change elsewhere in Europe. Knowledge about the country remained patchy as demonstrated in the entry for San Marino in the *Encyclopédie* which locates the Republic between Rome and Naples. Travellers' accounts of San Marino, including those of Joseph Addison and J. Gillies, tended to be superficial descriptions of the site and its people, sprinkled with the occasional historical fact, the Republic often used as a pretext for critical incursions against other governments and political systems. It was only in the nineteenth century that systematic examination of archival evidence began with the work of Melchiorre Delfico (1804) and Marino Fattori (1869).

70 **I Montefeltro e la Repubblica di San Marino.** (The Montefeltros and the Republic of San Marino.) Gino Franceschini. *Studi Romagnoli,* vol. 9 (1958), p. 35-65.

This article, based on a paper read at the 1957 conference of the Society of Romagnolo Studies, traces the relationship between the Counts of Montefeltro and San Marino from the thirteenth to the fourteenth century. This was a turbulent time as both were in dispute with the Catholic Church and were attempting to maintain their independence from Rome. The Counts of Montefeltro were eventually to become Dukes of Urbino, who in 1549 signed a defence treaty with the government of San Marino. The article includes the texts of some of the more important documents.

71 **Montegiardino: una comunità rurale tra '700 e '900.** (Montegiardino: a rural community from 1700 to 1900.) Cristoforo Buscarini. *Studi Sammarinesi,* vol. 1 (1984), p. 25-59. maps.

Montegiardino in the eighteenth and nineteenth centuries was a typical rural community based around an agricultural subsistence economy. This article gives a brief introduction to the village, before turning to demographics. The author examines the parish records for 1772 when the population was just 229. Other records are analysed, including the first official census, taken in 1865. The article ends with an examination of the data from the 1899 census, by which time there were 614 inhabitants. An appendix contains details of names, ages and addresses of individuals taken from the parish records of 1772, 1779, 1839 and 1860, and from the census of 1865. The article also reproduces maps of Montegiardino from 1775, 1823 and 1865. This represents the first part of a larger study by the author, the rest of which is to be published in later issues of *Studi Sammarinesi.*

72 **La Repubblica di San Marino durante l'êra napoleonica, 1796-1814.**
(The Republic of San Marino during the Napoleonic era, 1796-1814.)
Pina Rossini. *Libertas Perpetua: Museum*, year 3, no. 1
(Oct. 1934-April 1935), p. 106-26; year 3, no. 2 (April-Oct. 1935),
p. 64-73.

In 1797 French armies occupied much of Italy, but instead of invading San Marino,
the Republic's history and character were respected and Napoleon sent a message to
the Captains Regent stating that the country should be preserved as an example of
freedom. This article discusses San Marino's relationship with Napoleon and his
Italian puppet states and also with the Papacy, and traces local political and social
developments throughout the period.

73 **Il Risorgimento.** (The Risorgimento.)
Marco Pelliconi. In: *Storia illustrata della Repubblica di San Marino*.
San Marino: AIEP, 1985, p. 301-32. bibliog.

Pelliconi looks at the period from the Congress of Vienna of 1815, when the old order
of states in Italy was partially re-established at the end of the Napoleonic period, to
around 1870, by which time Italy was united as one kingdom but without
incorporating San Marino. The author concentrates on describing the economic and
social development of San Marino, its relations with the neighbouring Papal States,
the role of Antonio Onofri, public unrest, and Italian political asylum-seekers in the
Republic (Garibaldi among others). Other personalities discussed include Domenico
Maria Belzoppi, Giuseppe Bergonzi and Bartolomeo Borghesi. The article concludes
by summarizing the impact Italian unification had on San Marino. The text is well
illustrated with portraits and reproductions of important documents from the period.

74 **La Rivoluzione Francese e Napoleone: le ripercussioni a San
Marino.** (The French Revolution and Napoleon: repercussions in San
Marino.)
Pier Paolo Guardigli. In: *Storia illustrata della Repubblica di San
Marino*. San Marino: AIEP, 1985, p. 269-84. maps. bibliog.

This article begins by looking at the wider picture of Italy in the late eighteenth and
early nineteenth centuries. The old order was disappearing and new states were being
created by Napoleon, with much of north-western Italy, Tuscany and Latium being
incorporated into the French Empire. The author follows the correspondence of 1797
between San Marino and France, illustrating the degree to which Sanmarinese
independence seemed threatened. The crisis did not end until Napoleon personally
recognized the freedom of the Republic and ordered General Sahuguet to deliver
1,000 quintals of cereals as a sign of friendship. The influence of the Jacobin
movement on internal politics in San Marino is also considered in some detail by the
author. The article contains reproductions of several key documents held by the State
Archive (including the letter to the people of San Marino signed by Napoleon), maps,
portraits and a short bibliography.

75 **San Marino dopo la restaurazione, 1815-1821.** (San Marino after the
Restoration, 1815-21.)
Pina Rossini. *Libertas Perpetua: Museum,* year 4, no. 1
(Oct. 1935-April 1936), p. 180-7; year 4, no. 2 (April-Oct. 1936),
p. 97-106.

A detailed account of San Marino's relations with other European states and the
Catholic Church following Napoleon's defeat at Waterloo in 1815. This was a
particularly turbulent time for the Republic as Napoleon had effectively acted as its
guarantor, and there were fears that Austria might attempt to annex the country. As it
happened, Austrian troops did cross the borders, but the Congress of Vienna
confirmed San Marino's independence.

76 **Il Secolo dei lumi a San Marino: vicende politiche, economiche e
sociali della Repubblica nel Settecento.** (The Enlightenment in San
Marino: political, economic and social events in the Republic during the
eighteenth century.)
Pier Paolo Guardigli. In: *Biblioteca e Ricerca.* San Marino: AIEP,
1983, p. 49-62. (Quaderni del Dicastero Pubblica Istruzione e Cultura,
no. 2).

From the few sources available, the author of this article attempts to identify the social
events that characterized the eighteenth century in the Republic. The development of
the oligarchical state based on the medieval walled city of San Marino is traced, and
the urban and rural economies are compared.

77 **Sulla occupazione della Repubblica sammarinese operata dal
cardinale Giulio Alberoni.** (On the occupation of the Republic of San
Marino carried out by Cardinal Giulio Alberoni.)
Aurelio Muccioli. Naples, Italy: G. Nobile, 1869. 57p.

This collection of essays by A. Muccioli has Cardinal Alberoni's invasion and
occupation of San Marino as its theme. After looking at the character of the Cardinal,
the volume becomes a reply to various points made in the work of Stefano Bersani.
The latter proposes that the Cardinal's occupation of the Republic was justified;
Muccioli attempts to disprove this.

**La République de Saint-Marin: son histoire, sa constitution et son statut
international.** (The Republic of San Marino: its history, constitution and
international status.)
See item no. 115.

Appunti su Rovereta e la crisi sammarinese del 1957. (Notes on Rovereta
and the San Marino crisis of 1957.)
See item no. 116.

Cento anni di studi sulla Romagna, 1861-1961: bibliografia storica. (One
hundred years of studies on Romagna, 1861-1961: an historical
bibliography.)
See item no. 244.

Emigration

78 Changing patterns of migration in the Adriatic region.

P. Chatzer. *International Migration*, no. 26, part 2 (1988), p. 215-19.

This article discusses the changing patterns of migration in the Adriatic region, examining data from various countries including San Marino. Four types of population movements are identified: economically motivated (legal or clandestine), refugee (for resettlement), transient (ultimate resettlement in a third country), and return migration by former emigrants.

79 L'emigrazione. (Emigration.)

Pier Paolo Guardigli. In: *Storia illustrata della Repubblica di San Marino*. San Marino: AIEP, 1985, p. 365-80.

Guardigli focuses on the nineteenth and the early years of the twentieth century, a period of enormous demographic changes throughout Europe. In San Marino, the population doubled between 1818 and 1874 and this, combined with the Republic's lack of industry and more favourable economic conditions elsewhere, led to the impoverishment of sectors of the rural population and emigration. The article distinguishes between 'internal' emigration (i.e. to other parts of the Italian peninsula, usually happening during the winter months) and emigration abroad. The latter started towards the end of the nineteenth century, and by 1914 some 17.5 per cent of the population had emigrated abroad. With the advent of Fascism political reasons for emigrating were added to the economic ones.

80 San Marino fuori San Marino. (San Marino outside San Marino.)

Gemma Cavalleri. In: *Storia illustrata della Repubblica di San Marino*. San Marino: AIEP, 1985, p. 381-96.

Gives a short history of Sanmarinese emigration, from the first wave of worker emigrants at the turn of the century to the more recent repatriation trends and the emigration of the professional classes. It also examines the bilateral agreements and conventions regarding migration between San Marino and other countries (especially Italy, recipient of 60 per cent of the Sanmarinese emigrants) and looks at the Republic's diplomatic and consular representation as well as its participation in

Emigration

international organizations. Finally the social and cultural role of associations of San Marino citizens living abroad is examined as well as that of the Consulta, the assembly founded in 1979 which acts as a forum between the state and expatriate Sanmarinese communities, which has been instrumental to the adoption of important measures such as the granting of scholarships. The article includes various useful tables showing migration trends, the distribution of Sanmarinese emigrants, their numbers and social background.

Language and Dialect

81 **Dizionario degli etnici e dei toponimi italiani.** (Dictionary of Italian ethnic groups and place-names.)
  Teresa Cappello, Carlo Tagliavini.   Bologna, Italy: Pàtron, 1981. 641p.
The section on San Marino (p. 639-41) contains a list of settlement names and the correct designation for their inhabitants, indicating the local dialect form of these in a phonetic alphabet.

82 **L'italiano nelle regioni: lingua nazionale e identità regionali.** (Italian in the regions: national language and regional identity.)
  Edited by Francesco Bruni.   Turin, Italy: UTET, 1992. 1038p. bibliog.
  (La Nostra Lingua).
Bruni's major work looks at the development and current state of the language in all Italian-speaking areas of southern Europe. The chapter on Bologna and Romagna (p. 371-91) includes several references to historical texts originating in San Marino. The description of the regional variety of Italian today and its relationship with dialect is as valid for San Marino as it is for the rest of Romagna.

83 **Noterelle sul dialetto sammarinese.** (Notes on the Sanmarinese dialect.)
  Marino Rossi.   *Libertas Perpetua: Museum*, year 1, no. 1 (Jan.-March 1932), p. 70-1; year 1, no. 2 (April-Oct. 1932), p. 65-74; year 2, no. 1 (Oct. 1932-April 1934), p. 100-3.
A general introduction to the dialect of San Marino, taking examples not only from the spoken language, but also from literature. Two poems by the poet Pietro Rossi, both entitled *Canzone*, are printed with a parallel Italian translation and analysed linguistically.

84 **Proposta per una grafia letteraria della lingua romagnola.**
(Proposals for a literary spelling system of the Romagnolo language.)
Tolmino Baldassari.   Ravenna, Italy: Longo, 1979. 16p. (Studi di
Glottologia).

This slim volume proposes a standardized system for the writing of Romagnolo
dialects, such as those spoken in San Marino. The work is full of examples, including
a look at how other writers, such as Ercolani and Spallicci, have tackled the problem.

Religion

85   **La Chiesa e il movimento cattolico.** (The Church and the Catholic
Movement.)
Angelo Turchini.   In: *Storia illustrata della Repubblica di San Marino*.
San Marino: AIEP, 1985, p. 493-508. bibliog.

This article looks at the early years of the Catholic Movement in San Marino during
the first two decades of the twentieth century. The author looks at the role of
personalities such as Marino Nicolini and Don Michele Bucci, at organizations such as
the Opera dei Congressi and the Cassa Rurale di San Marino, and at debates that took
place in *Il Giovane Montefeltro*, *Il Titano*, *Sammarino* and other periodicals. The
organization of the Catholic Church in the Republic is described, whereby the parishes
have always been split between the two bishoprics of Rimini and Montefeltro. The
article contains photographs of key personalities and church buildings, as well as
reproductions of the title-pages of several contemporary periodicals.

86   **Ragguaglio dello stato, in cui era la Repubblica di S. Marino prima
della libera, e spontanea dedizione di que' Popoli alla Santa Sede.**
(Details of how the Republic of San Marino was the first to express
people's free and spontaneous devotion to the Holy See.)
Corpo del Magistrato.   Ravenna, Italy: Stamperia Camerale, 1739. 19p.

This early eighteenth-century expression of loyalty to the Papal See by the people of
San Marino gives a historical overview of the Republic's relations with the Roman
Catholic Church from earliest times. It is followed by a reply from Cardinal Alberoni
of Ravenna.

Health and Welfare

87   Cancer mortality in the Republic of San Marino.
E. M. S. Conti (et al.).   *International Journal of Epidemiology,* vol. 15,
no. 3 (1986), p. 420-23.
This article takes a historical look at the high occurrence of stomach cancer in the
Republic. Records for the years 1908-80 are examined, and stomach cancer is found to
be the most common cause of death, although in later years the survey discovers a
marked increase in cancers of the respiratory tract and the colon.

88   Dementia in subjects over 65 years of age in the Republic of San
Marino.
R. D'Alessandro (et al.).   *Journal of Psychiatry,* vol. 153 (1988),
p. 182-6.
These are the findings on dementia following a study on neurological conditions that
was performed in the Republic of San Marino by a team from the Institute of
Neurology of the University of Bologna. The authors made an intensive study of
subjects over sixty-five years of age living in the Republic, examining or collecting
information on all people born in 1898, 1903, 1908, 1913 and living in the Republic in
1985. Twenty-nine out of 488 were found to have mild to severe dementia. The
frequency of dementia increased progressively with age from 1.8 per cent among
sixty-seven-year-olds to 25 per cent among eighty-seven-year-olds. In women the
increase was due mainly to primary degenerative dementia, whereas in men other
types of dementia were involved. An association between severe auditory loss and
primary degenerative dementia was found.

89   The economic burden of headache: an epidemiological study in the
Republic of San Marino.
G. Benassi (et al.).   *Headache,* vol. 25, no. 9 (1986), p. 457-9.
This article studies the socio-economic effects of the high occurrence of headaches
among the San Marino population. In a sample of 514 people, 49.6 per cent are shown
to suffer from headaches, resulting in 338 days being taken off ill from work. The

article estimates that headaches cost the Republic some five thousand working days per year, or around five hundred million Italian lire.

90   **Epidemiology of headache in the Republic of San Marino.**
R. D'Alessandro (et al.).   *Journal of Neurology, Neurosurgery and Psychiatry,* vol. 51, no. 51 (1988), p. 21-7.

This article reports an epidemiological survey which examined a sample of 1,500 inhabitants over the age of seven in the mid-1980s. The survey found that 18 per cent of women and 9.3 per cent of men suffer from migraines. Severe headaches are experienced by 20.6 per cent of women and 12.2 per cent of men. The authors suggest that emotional stress, physical strain, lack of sleep and reactions to particular types of food or drink appear to be the main causes.

91   **Gastric cancer in San Marinese and their first degree relatives in San Marino and the USA: gastroscopic biopsy as an epidemiological tool.**
B. M. Schuman (et al.).   *Gastrointestinal Endoscopy,* vol. 33, no. 3 (1987), p. 224-6.

Inhabitants of San Marino display a particularly high rate of gastric cancer. This article reports on a population study which shows that around 36 per cent from a sample of 143 citizens were subject to this form of cancer. It also looks at people of San Marino origin living in Detroit, and shows that the phenomenon is repeated there.

92   **Prevalence of mental retardation related to fragile X syndrome and other chromosomal abnormalities in the Republic of San Marino.**
Sergio Cammarata (et al.).   *Developmental Medicine and Child Neurology,* vol. 30, no. 5 (Oct. 1988), p. 646-9.

This article presents the initial results of the first survey into chromosomal abnormality to have been carried out in southern Europe. The survey looked at 2,735 males aged between five and twenty years. Five cases of chromosomal abnormality were found, including one case of fragile X syndrome, where a six-year-old boy showed partial epilepsy and proved to have a large arachnoid cyst. The article is in English with French, German and Spanish summaries.

Politics

93 **L'Arringo conquistato: democrazia e socialismo nella Repubblica di San Marino, 1898-1906.** (The Arengo conquered: democracy and socialism in the Republic of San Marino, 1898-1906.)
Gianni Dordoni. San Marino: Edizioni del Titano, 1993. 190p. (L'Arengo).

Dordoni's monograph traces the development of liberalism in the second half of the nineteenth century, and the growth of the trade union movement and the Socialist Party. It gives the background to the referendum of 25 March 1906, a turning point in the political life of San Marino. The contribution of left-wing newspapers such as *Il Giovane Titano* (1880) and *Il Radicale* is examined as well as that of organizations such as the Società Unione di Mutuo Soccorso (founded in 1876).

94 **Aspetti della presenza del Borghesi nella vita pubblica sammarinese.** (Aspects of Borghesi's presence in the public life of San Marino.)
Cristoforo Buscarini. In: *Bartolomeo Borghesi, scienza e libertà: colloquio internazionale AIEGL.* Bologna, Italy: Pàtron, 1982, p. 239-88. (Studi e Storia, no. 1).

Bartolomeo Borghesi (1782-1860) was a leading writer on coins and epigrams, but was also a politician. Italian by birth, he spent much of his life in San Marino, which he saw as a haven of liberty in the difficult period leading up to the Risorgimento. After becoming a Sanmarinese citizen in 1818, he became increasingly involved in the Republic's political problems. In this conference paper, the writer traces Borghesi's political career, using documentation found in the Archivio di Stato.

95 **Democracy in San Marino.**
D. W. King. *Contemporary Review*, vol. 216, no. 1248 (Jan. 1970), p. 6-9, 22.

Concerned principally with political parties, this article discusses how they have fared in past elections in the light of the general election of 7 September 1969, when the Christian Democrats retained power with a slightly reduced number of seats. There is also a brief introduction to the way in which the country is governed.

96 **Il Fascismo.** (Fascism.)
Angela Colombini, Francesca Michelotti. In: *Storia illustrata della Repubblica di San Marino*. San Marino: AIEP, 1985, p. 541-56. bibliog.

In essence, this article gives a political history of the Republic from 1922, when the Fascist Party was founded, until the end of the Second World War. The authors consider the reasons for the rise of Fascism in San Marino, and examine how Sanmarinese Fascism differed from that in Italy. They describe the influence of the brothers Manlio Gozi (1889-1968) and Giuliano Gozi (1894-1955), who between them held a considerable number of posts in the party and government, and who were both Captains Regent several times. The article looks at opposition to the Fascist régime, including the failed coup attempt of 1933, and the Republic's foreign policy during this period. The fall of Fascism in 1943-45 is also described. There are several photographs and a special section on the Rimini–San Marino railway line.

97 **Le forze politiche dall'Arengo al fascismo.** (Political forces from the Arengo to Fascism.)
Pier Paolo Poggio. In: *Storia illustrata della Repubblica di San Marino*. San Marino: AIEP, 1985, p. 509-24. bibliog.

This article covers the period 1906 (when full authority was returned to the Arengo) to 1926 (when the Fascists implemented a new electoral law). It looks at the political struggle between the democrats (socialists, republicans and 'progressives') and the conservatives, at the successes and failures of the government, and at the rise of Fascism. The article contains a large number of photographs of key political figures from the period.

98 **Joining the Christian Democrats in a ruling coalition.**
Alberto Mino. *World Marxist Review*, vol. 30, no. 7 (July 1987), p. 79-84.

This article takes the form of an interview with Alberto Mino, the head of the Communist Party External Political Affairs Commission, in which he talks about the Communist Party's experience of power sharing; first with the Socialists and then with the Christian Democrats. There is a detailed account of the government crisis of mid-1986, and an insight into the involvement of the Communist Party in San Marino society.

99 **Pietro Franciosi.**
Marco Pelliconi. In: *Storia illustrata della Repubblica di San Marino*. San Marino: AIEP, 1985, p. 525-40. bibliog.

Pelliconi's article looks at the life and work of Pietro Franciosi (1864-1935), Sanmarinese politician, public administrator, educationalist and scholar. It looks at his early life, his involvement with the Società Unione e Mutuo Soccorso (of which he was president from 1895 to 1917), and the important role he played in politics as the country's leading democrat. It also briefly describes the last years of his life in Rimini after being forced into exile by the Fascist government. The article contains several photographs and concludes with a bibliography of works by Franciosi.

100 **Political parties of the world.**
Compiled and edited by Alan J. Day, Henry W. Degenhardt. London:
Longman, 1984. 2nd ed. 602p. (Keesing's Reference Publications).

The section on San Marino (p. 388-90) gives details in English of the seven political
parties active in the Republic in the 1980s. Information given includes addresses,
names of leaders, history, political orientation, membership numbers and publications.
A brief introduction describes the system of government and distribution of seats in
the Great and General Council.

101 **San Marino: l'idea della Repubblica.** (San Marino: the concept of
Republic.)
Giovanni Spadolini. Florence, Italy: Le Monnier, 1989. 129p.
(Quaderni della Nuova Antologia, no. 38).

Based on a presentation made by the Italian politician Giovanni Spadolini in 1989
before San Marino's Great and General Council, this work traces the political
development of the country from medieval commune to twentieth-century republic.
The second part looks at the connections between San Marino and Pasquale Villari,
the Italian historian and politician (1826-1917).

102 **Storia del Partito fascista sammarinese.** (History of the San Marino
Fascist Party.)
Anna Lisa Carlotti. Milan, Italy: Celuc, 1973. 260p. bibliog.
(Ricerche, no. 31).

This article provides a history of the San Marino Fascist Party from its beginnings
until its final demise caused by the Allied invasion of 1943. Sections deal with the
country's political situation at the turn of the century, organized opposition and the
Party's relations with the outside world.

103 **La tradizione politica di San Marino: dalle origini
dell'indipendenza al pensiero politico di Pietro Franciosi.** (The
political tradition of San Marino: from the beginnings of independence
to the political thoughts of Pietro Franciosi.)
Edited by Elisabetta Righi Iwanejko. San Marino: Il Lavoro
Editoriale, 1988. 613p. (Biblioteca e Ricerca. Quaderni del Dicastero
Pubblica Istruzione e Cultura, no. 4).

This substantial volume contains twenty-seven papers presented at a conference on the
development of San Marino's political independence from earliest times to the
beginning of the twentieth century. Papers in the first and second sections look at
issues such as urban and rural society, sovereignty claims by the Holy See, foreign
relations, anarchy and socialism, and the economic situation. The third part of the
volume is devoted to Sanmarinese politician Pietro Franciosi, his life, his political and
historical works, and the impact he made on politics and institutions in the Republic
today. The conference was organized by the Department of Education and Culture in
collaboration with the State Library.

104 **V avangarde bor'by trudiashchikhsia San' Marino.** (In the
vanguard of the struggle of the workers of San Marino.)
Ermenegildo Gasperoni. *Voprosy istorii KPSS* (USSR), vol. 8 (1981),
p. 103-4.

The author, President of the Communist Party of San Marino, recalls his own personal
struggle as a Communist and the formation and development of his party. Gasperoni
left San Marino in 1924 and spent the next sixteen years in contact with communist
organizations throughout Europe, including a lengthy period with the international
brigades during the Spanish Civil War. He returned to the Republic in 1940 with the
intention of establishing an independent communist party. This was set up on 7 July
1941 and the Party became legal in 1945, and by 1957 more than one in ten of the
Republic's 14,000 population were members. The San Marino Communist Party
became the party of government in the elections of 1978.

Nascita del movimento operaio e socialista. (The birth of the socialist
workers' movement.)
See item no. 105.

**Bibliografia delle fonti sulla costituzione di movimenti, associazioni,
partiti politici e su aspetti della questione sociale della Repubblica di San
Marino tra il 1860 e il 1924: i materiali della Biblioteca di Stato.**
(Bibliography of sources on the establishment of movements, associations
and political parties, and of social issues in the Republic of San Marino from
1860 to 1924: the collections of the State Library.)
See item no. 241.

Trade Unions and the Labour Movement

105 **Nascita del movimento operaio e socialista.** (The birth of the
socialist workers' movement.)
Marco Pellicoli. In: *Storia illustrata della Repubblica di San Marino.*
San Marino: AIEP, 1985, p. 397-428. bibliog.

In the latter part of the nineteenth century, following on from political changes in Italy
resulting from its reunification, Sanmarinese citizens became increasing concerned
with their country's problems. Power was still concentrated in the hands of a small
number of families, there were few public services and the economy was in a mess.
This article describes these problems and shows how they led to the birth of the
socialist movement. The origins, development and activities of organizations such as
the Società Unione e Mutuo Soccorso (Unity and Mutual Aid Society), the Cassa di
Risparmio di San Marino (San Marino Savings Bank) and the San Marino Socialist
Party are discussed. The author looks at the influence of printing and publishing on
political debate after its introduction in 1879, with titles such as *Il Giovane Titano, La
Lotta* and *Il Radicale* being examined in detail. The role of the socialist thinker Pietro
Franciosi is also considered, and political events leading up to the workers' protests of
1900 are outlined. The article contains a large number of facsimiles of periodical title-
pages, manifestos and political posters, as well as contemporary photographs. It
includes a bibliography.

106 **Le origini del movimento operaio e socialista a San Marino.**
(The origins of the socialist workers' movement in San Marino.)
Marco Pelliconi. In: *Biblioteca e Ricerca.* San Marino: AIEP, 1983,
p. 113-35. bibliog. (Quaderni del Dicastero Pubblica Istruzione e
Cultura, no. 2).

The socio-political situation in San Marino at the end of the nineteenth century was far
from satisfactory. Large numbers of people were having to emigrate to find work and
a significant proportion of the remainder were still working the land using antiquated
techniques. Added to this, there was a ruling élite that appeared to be unable to
respond to the needs of the working classes, and there were large numbers of Italian
political exiles. Against this background, organizations such as the Società Socialista

Anarchica Rivoluzionaria Sammarinese (San Marino Revolutionary Anarchic Socialist Society) were founded, and links were established with various Italian working-class and socialist organizations. This article traces the development of these organizations, principally through the literature they produced. Photographs of key personalities are reproduced at the end, together with manifestos and pages from important newsletters and papers of the period.

107 **La Società Unione e Mutuo Soccorso.** (The Unity and Mutual Aid
      Society.)
      Pier Paolo Guardigli, Stefano Nespolesi. In: *Storia illustrata della
      Repubblica di San Marino.* San Marino: AIEP, 1985, p. 429-44.
      bibliog.

This article begins with a description of social conditions in San Marino in the mid-nineteenth century and of the development of mutual aid societies in Italy. The author traces the origins of the Società Unione e Mutuo Soccorso di San Marino back to a 'unione' of young citizens in Borgo Maggiore and San Marino city that began in 1874. He follows its development into the Società in 1876, and the setting up of the Cassa di Risparmio di San Marino (San Marino Savings Bank) in 1881. Many of the activities of the Società are described, including the opening of a grain store in 1890 to provide members and non-members with cereals at a controlled price with payment by instalments, and its involvement in the Universal Exhibition of 1900 in Paris. The chapter contains contemporary photographs, facsimiles of announcements and other documents, and a list of presidents of the Società.

L'Arringo conquistato: democrazia e socialismo nella Repubblica di San Marino, 1898-1906. (The Arengo conquered: democracy and socialism in the Republic of San Marino, 1898-1906.)
See item no. 93.

V avangarde bor'by trudiashchikhsia San' Marino. (In the vanguard of the struggle of the workers of San Marino.)
See item no. 104.

Constitution

108 Constitutions of nations.
Amos J. Peaslee. The Hague, Netherlands: Martinus Nijhoff, 1968.
3rd rev. ed. 4 vols in 7 parts.

This substantial work cites the constitutions of most independent states. The chapter on San Marino begins on p. 788, and gives an English translation of the Electoral Law of 1958 (Legge elettorale approvata dal Consiglio Grande e Generale ... il 29 dicembre 1958). Issues covered in the text of the act include the requirements for voters, formation of electoral lists and the electoral college, and the procedures to be followed before voting can commence.

109 Constitutions of the countries of the world.
Edited by Albert P. Blaustein, Gilbert H. Flanz. New York: Oceana, [196-?]- . 21 vols. bibliog.

This is a loose-leaf work, currently in twenty volumes with a supplement, that continues to be updated. It aims to give the constitutions of all independent states in the world, with English translations where appropriate. The section on San Marino is in binder no. 14, and is by Gilbert H. Flanz. In the introduction he states that the foundations of the Republic's 'impressive constitutional tradition' can be traced back more than a thousand years. The section does not contain any texts, but there is a constitutional chronology and a short bibliography.

110 Una costituzione straniera in Italia: la costituzione della Repubblica di San Marino. (A foreign constitution in Italy: the constitution of the Republic of San Marino).
Giorgio Sozzi. Thesis, University of Florence, 1983. 248p. bibliog.

Sozzi's thesis is divided into three chapters. The first gives a short history of the Republic, while the second describes the development of its main constitutional bodies, their peculiar characteristics and respective powers. The third, and most substantial, chapter describes the evolution of the constitution of San Marino and explains the character and present powers of its constitutional bodies.

111 **Democracy at San Marino.**
William Miller. *History: the Quarterly Journal of the Historical Association*, new series, vol. 7, no. 25 (April 1922), p. 1-16.
Constitutional practice was broken in 1920 when the two Captains Regent remained in office at the end of their six-month tour of duty, on the basis that there were no other suitable candidates. This article reports these events and describes the development of the constitution from earliest times.

112 **Evoluzione storica della costituzione di S. Marino.** (Historical evolution of the constitution of San Marino.)
Alberto Garbelotto. Milan, Italy: Gastaldi, 1956. 103p.
Garbelotto's work first describes the various statutes of the 'commune' of San Marino, beginning in the thirteenth century, and goes on to trace the development of the current constitution, including the alterations made before and after the Second World War. There is a description of the principal institutions of the Republic, the Captains Regent and the councils, and the 1939 Convention of Friendship with Italy. The final chapter considers the future of San Marino and the possible constitutional developments.

113 **Les petits états d'Europe: Andorre, Liechtenstein, Monaco, Saint-Marin.** (The little states of Europe: Andorra, Liechtenstein, Monaco, San Marino.)
Duke Astraudo. Paris: [n.p.], 1938. 3rd ed. 125p. map. bibliog.
The section on San Marino is on pages 93-124. After a brief description of the country and its history, the main part concentrates on the Republic's constitution and its international relations. There is also a section on the Orders of Merit (with illustrations of two crosses). The work is also of interest as a historical document for its description of the newly opened electric railway line between San Marino and Rimini and for the author's pro-Mussolini views.

114 **Problematiche istituzionali: ordinamento e istituti costituzionali della Repubblica di San Marino.** (Institutional problems: law and constitutional institutions in the Republic of San Marino.)
Renzo Bonelli. In: *Storia illustrata della Repubblica di San Marino*. San Marino: AIEP, 1985, p. 717-32. bibliog.
San Marino does not have a single Constitution and its constitutional laws are to be found, instead, in various texts, both ancient (the Statutes of 1600) and modern (the Declaration of the Rights of Citizens, 1974). This article discusses the various constitutional bodies of the Republic, explaining their structure and functions.

115 **La République de Saint-Marin: son histoire, sa constitution et son statut international.** (The Republic of San Marino: its history, constitution and international status.)
Duke Astraudo. San Marino: Imprimerie della Balda, 1932. 20p. bibliog.

Although the text of this study was re-used and expanded in item no. 113 (q.v.), this edition is of interest for the quality of its illustrations. These include facsimiles of the *Placito Feretrano* and a letter by Napoleon. There are also views of San Marino which include the construction of the tunnel at Montale and the newly built railway station.

Government

116 **Appunti su Rovereta e la crisi sammarinese del 1957.** (Notes on
Rovereta and the San Marino crisis of 1957.)
Giorgio P. Sozzi. *Studi Romagnoli*, vol. 35 (1984), p. 453-80.
The post-war years were difficult for San Marino. There were a series of economic
disputes with Italy. The Fascists, who had run the country until the end of the Second
World War, were now banned from office, and there was no clear alternative party of
government. The elections of 1951 gave the Christian Democrats a slight majority, but
by 1955 public opinion had changed and the Communists were in power, causing
concern abroad. By 1957 the economic and political situation had still not been
resolved, and an alternative provisional government set up at Rovereta (near Falciano)
was immediately recognized by both Italy and the United States. This article traces the
development of the crisis, quoting various decrees, press releases and media reports of
the time.

117 **L'Arengo.** (The Arengo.)
Pier Paolo Poggio.   In: *Storia illustrata della Repubblica di San
Marino*.   San Marino: AIEP, 1985, p. 445-60. bibliog.
An 'arengo' (or 'arringo') is an assembly of heads of families that comes together to
make legislative and executive decisions relating to the public life of a medieval
commune. In San Marino, the Arengo had run the country until the Consiglio Principe
(or Consiglio Grande) had gradually taken over in the sixteenth century. From this
point on it was largely ceremonial. This essay examines the history of the Arengo,
how it functioned, and how it lost its power to the Consiglio – a body that consisted of
unelected landed nobility. It also examines the long political campaign of 1902-6 for
its return in response to poor social conditions, government corruption and economic
crisis. The piece ends with the referendum of 1906 when the citizens of San Marino
voted to return sovereignty to the Arengo and convened its first full meeting for 350
years. The text is accompanied by a number of photographs and reproductions of
documents, pamphlets and front-pages of contemporary newspapers.

118   **I castelli.** (The castles.)
Gabriella Lorenzi, Silva Savoretti.   In: *Storia illustrata della
Repubblica di San Marino*.   San Marino: AIEP, 1985, p. 925-56.
bibliog.

This article is divided into two parts. The first traces the origins and historical
development of territorial settlements in San Marino. In the Middle Ages the territory
was divided into ten *gualdarie* (zones) which in the fifteenth century became
parrocchie (parishes). When in 1463 the Republic annexed the territories of
Fiorentino, Montegiardino, Faetano and Serravalle these were granted partial
autonomy, each having its own captain; eventually other territories of the Republic
adopted the same titles. In 1925 the San Marino territory was divided into ten zones
(*castelli*), roughly following the divisions of the former *parrocchie*, their captains
nominated by the Captains Regent. In 1945 the functions of the Captain were taken
over by the *Giunta di Castello*, a local council with a number of members determined
by the population of each *castello*. The second part of the article gives a short history
and description of each of the present nine *castelli*, namely Acquaviva, Borgo
Maggiore, Chiesanuova, Domagnano, Faetano, Fiorentino, Montegiardino, Castello di
Città and Serravalle.

119   **Organi istituzionali e amministrazione pubblica.** (Institutional
bodies and public administration.)
In: *Guida Titano: annuario amministrativo ed economico della
Repubblica di San Marino. 1994-1995*.   San Marino: Edizioni del
Titano, 1994, sections 1-145.

These pages give contact names, addresses, telephone and facsimile numbers for all of
San Marino's government departments, commissions, local authorities (*castelli*),
schools, museums, libraries and all other state-run bodies. The same information is
also given for representatives of foreign governments whether based inside or outside
the territory. Several of the sections are preceded by a brief introduction explaining
the responsibilities or characteristics of the body or institution concerned. The text is
in both Italian and English.

Libro d'oro della Repubblica di San Marino. (Social register of the
Republic of San Marino.)
See item no. 46.

Law and Order

Legal system

120 **Kime's international law directory.**
Edited and compiled by James M. Matthews. Carlisle, England:
Kime's International Law Directory, 1792- . annual. 1 vol.

Gives a brief history of San Marino's legal system and information on professional
education. It also explains professional designations, explaining the difference
between an *avvocato*, a *procuratore*, a *notaio* and a *coadiutore*. It lists fifteen
practitioners in Borgo Maggiore, San Marino and Serravalle.

121 **Leges statutae Reipublicae Sancti Marini.** (Legal statutes of the
Republic of San Marino.)
San Marino Government. Florence, Italy: Ex Cooperativa
Typographia, 1895. 245p.

The official collection of legal statutes in force during the second half of the
nineteenth century, as ordered to be printed on the 8 May 1893. The texts are in Latin
with a parallel Italian translation. The volume contains detailed subject indexes in
both languages.

122 **Raccolta delle leggi e decreti della Repubblica di San Marino.**
(Collection of the laws and decrees of the Republic of San Marino.)
Consiglio Principe e Sovrano. Città di Castello [i.e. San Marino]:
S. Lapi, 1900. 650p.

This is the 'first official edition' of the legal codes of San Marino as in force in 1900.
The Constitutional and Civil codes are in Latin, but the remainder of the volume –
containing Fiscal Law, Procedural Law, Penal Law, Administrative Law, International
Law and Heraldic Law – is in Italian. The section on International Law includes the
text of a treaty between the Republic and the United Kingdom concerning the
extradition of criminals (1899).

123 **La Repubblica di San Marino e gli statuti del 1352-53.**
(The Republic of San Marino and the statutes of 1352-53.)
Francesco Balsimelli. *Libertas Perpetua: Museum*, year 6, no. 2
(April-Oct. 1938), p. 33-48; year 7, no. 1 (Oct. 1939-April 1939),
p. 27-51; year 7, no. 2 (April-Oct. 1939), p. 55-90.

The 1350s were difficult years; San Marino's independence was repeatedly threatened, and nearby feudal lords were attempting to gain control. This article gives a historical background to these events, then goes on to look at the 1352-53 statutes, a work in which all the Republic's laws were collated for the first time. The article ends with a transcription of the text and a photograph of the first page.

124 **Staatsangehörigkeitsrecht von Andorra, Liechtenstein, Monaco, San Marino, der Vatikan-Stadt.** (The law of nationality in Andorra, Liechtenstein, Monaco, San Marino and the Vatican City.)
Hellmuth Hecker. Frankfurt, Germany: Alfred Metzner, 1958. 110p.
(Sammlung geltender Staatsangehörigkeitsgesetze, no. 21).

The author devotes pages 88-95 to San Marino. After a brief summary of San Marino's legal and constitutional history, he concentrates on nationality law. This is based on three main sources: common law, statutes and special laws. Under common law any child of a San Marino citizen is automatically a citizen of the Republic regardless of where born. Nationality can be lost only by a citizen's own stated desire – the government cannot remove citizenship or prevent anyone from renouncing citizenship. Under statutes, six years' uninterupted residence with good behaviour can entitle foreigners to apply for citizenship. Special laws passed in 1907, 1914 and 1945 (in force for one year, fifteen days and one year respectively) affected those who had lived for between ten and twenty years in San Marino. The texts of the relevant statutes and the special laws mentioned above are given in the final section.

125 **Testo del progetto del codice penale della Repubblica di San Marino.** (Text of the project for a penal code for the Republic of San Marino.)
Professor Zuppetta. Naples, Italy: Tipografia della Regia Università, 1867. 155, 136p.

In 1859 Professor Zuppetta was asked by the Sanmarinese government to compile a new penal code. This annotated draft is the result of his work and covers all aspects of law. Some subsequent amendments are included. The code was ratified in September 1865.

126 **La tutela del minore nel nuovo diritto di famiglia: osservazioni di diritto comparato.** (The custody of minors in the new family law: observations on comparative law.)
San Marino: Istituto Giuridico Sammarinese, 1989. 168p.

This volume consists of papers presented at a conference on the custody of minors in the light of recent reforms to family law, which was organized by the Republic's legal institute in 1987. The seven papers included describe the rights of individuals and families, discuss the need for reform, and assess the impact of the changes. The text of laws no. 49 to 51 of 26 April 1986 ('Reform of family law', 'Rules on civil status, acts of marriage and identification of persons' and 'Repeal of Article 225 of the Penal Code – Adultery') are given on pages 147-68.

127   **Union list of West European legal literature: publications held by libraries in Oxford, Cambridge and London.**
Compiled by Kathleen Hedberg.   London: Institute of Advanced Legal Studies, 1966. 426p. (Institute of Advanced Legal Studies Union Catalogue, no. 5).
There is a page on San Marino, giving references to law reports and legislation.

Guide mondial des paradis fiscaux. (World guide to tax havens.)
See item no. 147.

Tax law and exchange control in the Republic of San Marino.
See item no. 150.

Police and armed forces

128   **I corpi militari della Repubblica di San Marino.** (Military bodies in the Republic of San Marino.)
Elisabetta Righi Iwanejko.   In: *Storia illustrata della Repubblica di San Marino.*   San Marino: AIEP, 1985, p. 189-204. bibliog.
Iwanejko looks at defence forces in San Marino from the Middle Ages to the mid-twentieth century. There are sections on the crossbow, including the medieval Palio of crossbowmen and harquebusiers, and the general organization of military forces in which bodies such as the Corpo della Milizia, the Corpo dei Gendarmi, the Guardia Civica and the Genio Pompieri amongst others are discussed. A facsimile of an essay on military uniforms taken from the *Corriere dei Piccoli* (no. 26, 1934) is inserted, and the text of the 1600 statute on the privileges of the militia is given. The article is well illustrated with photographs of soldiers in ceremonial uniform, and contains a short bibliography.

129   **La Repubblica di San Marino.** (The Republic of San Marino.)
Fernando Amedeo Rubini.   *Rivista Militare*, vol. 100, no. 3 (May-June 1977), p. 104-5.
This brief article gives a historical outline of armed forces in the Republic, from earliest times to date. It concludes with a short description of relations between San Marino and Italy.

130 **San Marino e le sue forze armate.** (San Marino and its armed forces.)
Giorgio P. Sozzi. *Studi Romagnoli*, vol. 37 (1986), p. 269-83.

This article looks at the Republic's armed forces from a legislative point of view. It concentrates principally on the gendarmerie, from its formation in the eighteenth century, to its role in the constitutional crisis of 1957, when a provisional government was established in Rovereta. The text is supported by lengthy extracts from law and government decrees, some of which are in Latin without translation.

Foreign Relations

131 **Exchange of notes between the Government of the United Kingdom of Great Britain and Northern Ireland and the Republic of San Marino concerning a payment made to San Marino in respect of war damage, Florence and San Marino, July 17/22, 1961.**
Foreign Office. London: HMSO, 1961. 5p. (Command Paper, 1571/1961; Treaty Series, no. 115/1961).
On 26 June 1944, Britain's Desert Air Force bombed the city of San Marino. In this document, the British government disclaims all liability for damage, but makes a payment of £80,000 as a gesture of sympathy for the suffering caused.

132 **Little states in a world of powers: a study of the conduct of foreign affairs by Andorra, Liechtenstein, Monaco and San Marino.**
Joseph Hirsch Rogatnick. PhD thesis, University of Pennsylvania, 1976. 389p.
Examines the diplomacy of these four 'little states' and analyses the processes and methods that they have adopted for dealing with larger members of the international community. The thesis is divided in two parts, entitled 'descriptive' and 'analytic'. The first part describes the prevailing environments in these countries and sketches their historical development as states and their emergence as members of the international community. The second part examines in detail their character of statehood under international law and analyses their functional arrangements with contiguous powers and their relations with international organizations. It also examines how the foreign policies of these states are implemented given the constraints imposed by their very small size.

Les petits états d'Europe: Andorre, Liechtenstein, Monaco, Saint-Marin.
(The little states of Europe: Andorra, Liechtenstein, Monaco, San Marino.)
See item no. 113.

Organi istituzionali e amministrazione pubblica. (Institutional bodies and
public administration.)
See item no. 119.

Economy, Trade and Industry

Economy

133 **Ambiente, insediamenti, agricoltura e industria fra XVIII e XX secolo: brevi note di storia economica sammarinese.** (Environment, settlements, agriculture and industry from the eighteenth to the twentieth centuries: brief notes on San Marino's economic history.) Pier Paolo Guardigli. *Studi Sammarinesi*, vol. 5 (1988), p. 43-66. maps.

Guardigli begins with a geographical description of the land and then describes urban and rural human habitation patterns, before looking at demography during the last two centuries. The development of the rural economy is studied in detail, with sections on arable and livestock farming. Industry and business, from medieval craftsmen to late twentieth-century tourism, are also examined. The article includes a number of charts and maps illustrating changing demographic and agricultural situations.

134 **L'economia.** (The economy.) Antonio Corattoni. In: *Storia illustrata della Repubblica di San Marino.* San Marino: AIEP, 1985, p. 685-718. bibliog.

This article looks at the Sanmarinese economy during the last two centuries. It begins by describing social conditions in the nineteenth century and lists the economic activities which were being carried out, from markets and fairs to workshops and small factories. The second part considers the role played by government in the country's economy during the twentieth century, concentrating on the Fascist period, economic reconstruction since the Second World War, and state revenue during the 1960s and 1970s.

135 **Emilia Romagna.**
Financial Times (20 May 1991), p. 21-3. map.

A survey examining affluence in the region and the rise in social problems, the economy, banking, the cooperative movement and the food industry. There is a section on San Marino.

136 **Relazione al bilancio di previsione per l'Esercito finanziario.**
(Forward budget report of the Financial Department.)
Segretaria di Stato per le Finanze e il Bilancio.   San Marino:
The Segretaria, 1980- . annual.

The annual budget details the Government's planned expenditure, broken down by department. It gives a good insight into priorities and projects in hand at the time.

137 **Terre e torri: per una storia economica e sociale della Repubblica di San Marino.** (Lands and towers: a social and economic history of the Republic of San Marino).
Pier Paolo Guardigli.   San Marino: Edizioni del Titano, 1992. 158p.
(La Città Felice).

This volume brings together the author's writings on the economic and social evolution of San Marino's territory, tracing the development of its economy from its rural origins to the late development of industry in the twentieth century. There are two sections, the first dealing with general social and economic aspects from the Middle Ages to the present, while the second concentrates on more specific topics, such as viticulture and oenology; sanitation and the outburst of the cholera epidemic in 1855; the 'torri colombaie' [dovecots]; aspects of rural economy in the Malatesta Castle at Serravalle; and the role of watermills in the nineteenth century.

Europe's micro-states.
See item no. 17.

Trade

138 **Attività economiche.** (Economic activity.)
In: *Guida Titano: annuario amministrativo ed economico della Repubblica di San Marino. 1994-1995.*   San Marino: Edizioni del Titano, 1994, sections 213-62.

These pages contain a directory of Sanmarinese commercial companies. Each entry gives details of the firm's contact details, principal business, registration numbers and turnover. The sections are arranged by product types. The text is in Italian and English.

139 **Decision no. 2-4/92 of the EEC–San Marino Cooperation Committee of 22 December 1992.**
Official Journal of the EC, no. L42 (19 Feb. 1993), p. 23-36.

The texts of three key decisions of the EEC–San Marino Cooperation Committee are reproduced in this issue of the *Official Journal*. Decision no. 2 (92/102/EEC) concerns the laws, regulations and administrative provisions applicable to customs matters in the Community to be adopted by the Republic of San Marino. Decision no. 3 (92/103/EEC) looks at the arrangements for the provision of mutual assistance, and Decision no. 4 (92/104/EEC) concerns the method of implementation of the Interim Agreement, and the procedures for forwarding goods to San Marino. The summary states that it was agreed to postpone the implementation of Decision no. 4 until April 1993, to allow San Marino sufficient time to introduce new procedures. A corrigendum to this decision is to be found in *Official Journal of the EC*, no. L89 (6 April 1994), p. 32.

140 **Doing business in Italy.**
[United States]: Price Waterhouse, 1993. 244p.

Italy is, of course, San Marino's principal trading partner, and many businesses take little account of the border when carrying out commercial activities. For this reason, and because of the country's limited resources, the Republic's business laws and practices reflect those of its neighbour. It is also likely that anyone intending to do business in San Marino will need to do business with Italy as part of the process. This handy guide is ideal as a first point of reference. The laws and practices concerning imports/exports, investment, finance, regulation, accounting principles, industrial relations and tax are all concisely explained. There is also a broad-brush description of the Italian business environment.

141 **Interim agreement on trade and customs union between the European Economic Community and the Republic of San Marino.**
Official Journal of the EC, no. L359 (9 Dec. 1992), p. 14-21.

This agreement between the Council of the European Communities and San Marino came into force in December 1992. It establishes a customs union within the terms of the Common Customs Tariff and establishes a Cooperation Committee to administer the treaty. Article 7 of the agreement allows the EC to act on behalf of the Republic of San Marino by carrying out customs clearance formalities at the Italian cities of Livorno, Ravenna, Rimini, Forlì and Trieste. The preliminaries state that the agreement will need ratifying by national parliaments which will delay its enforcement.

Industry and crafts

142 **Cave e scalpellini: dall'epoca di Marino al XIX secolo.** (Caves and
stonecutters: from the time of Saint Marinus to the nineteenth century.)
Maria Pedini Angelini. In: *Storia illustrata della Repubblica di San
Marino*. San Marino: AIEP, 1985, p. 349-64.

Angelini traces the work of the stonecutters from Saint Marinus, traditionally a
stonecutter himself, to the twentieth century. Unlike artisans in Italian medieval states
the San Marino stonecutters did not belong to a corporation and, consequently, there is
no mention of their conditions of work in the Statutes of the Republic. During the
Renaissance they worked in other parts of the Italian peninsula, an indication both of
their fame and also of their need to seek work elsewhere. In the nineteenth century
their work was much admired at the various World Fairs while at home their main
work was the neoclassical basilica (1825-38) which replaced the Romanesque parish
church, the Palazzo del Governo (inaugurated in 1894) and the cemetery of Montalbo.
At the end of the nineteenth century stonecutters played a leading part in the
development of the Syndicalist movement in San Marino, but poverty and lack of
regular employment at home meant that, in the early years of the twentieth century,
large numbers were forced to emigrate. The article includes brief accounts of the work
of some leading artisans such as Carlo Reffi, Mansueto Mariotti and Romeo
Balsimelli.

143 **La cultura materiale: i segni dell'artigianato e dell'industria.**
(Material culture: traces of craft and industry.)
Giorgio Pedrocco. In: *Storia illustrata della Repubblica di San
Marino*. San Marino: AIEP, 1985, p. 877-92. bibliog.

This article takes a chronological look at the development of crafts and industry in San
Marino from earliest times to the present day. It begins with stonecutting, describing
how the workers organized themselves and their work, and goes on to consider
nineteenth-century watermills (of which the author lists eighteen), the establishment
of a gunpowder industry, and the arrival of industrialization. The last sections look at
the development of industrial zones, such as the one around Dogana and Serravalle,
and the growing importance of tourism. Photographs of significant industrial buildings
accompany the text.

144 **La tradizione sammarinese dei lapicidi.** (The Sanmarinese tradition
of stonemasonry.)
Francesco Balsimelli. *Libertas Perpetua: Museum*, year 5, no. 2
(Oct. 1937-April 1938), p. 76-88.

Balsimelli outlines the history of stonemasonry in San Marino from the 1400s to 1937.
There are portraits of the principal late nineteenth- and early twentieth-century
masons, and illustrations of their work.

Finance and Banking

145   Banche, società finanziarie e di assicurazioni. (Banks, financial and insurance companies.)
In: *Guida Titano: annuario amministrativo ed economico della Repubblica di San Marino. 1994-1995.*   San Marino: Edizioni del Titano, 1994, sections 158-65.

Details of San Marino's five banking organizations, their regulatory body (Inspectorate for Credit and Foreign Currency), and a variety of finance and insurance companies are given in these sections of this general guide. In some cases just contact names, addresses and numbers are quoted; in others there is a brief summary of the role of the organization. The text is principally in Italian, but some English translations are also given.

146   European finance and investment: offshore centres.
Financial Times (28 Feb. 1992), p. 9-11. map. tables.

A survey examining the paradoxes of the offshore financial centre. It compares regulations in a number of countries, including San Marino.

147   Guide mondial des paradis fiscaux. (World guide to tax havens.)
André Beauchamp.   Paris: Grasset, 1985. rev. ed. 778p.

The section on San Marino (p. 669-77) provides background information for individuals seeking tax havens. There are brief sections on the geography, population, means of communication and the political system, and more extensive ones giving financial and legal information.

148   Il sistema bancario e finanziario sammarinese. (The Sanmarinese banking and financial system.)
Alberto Chezzi, Marino Albani.   Rimini, Italy: Maggioli, 1991. 111p.

Includes a short historical outline of the monetary conventions between Italy and San Marino. The first two, in 1862 and 1864, allowed San Marino to mint coins that would

53

have circulation in Italy, while the Friendship and Good Neighbourliness Convention in 1939 established the customs union and the total currency and monetary integration between the two countries. The banking system of San Marino is also described, with a detailed description of the functions of the Istituto di Credito Sammarinese (which is, in effect, the Central Bank of the Republic). The texts of the body of legislation on banking – until recently limited to only a few clauses of the Friendship and Good Neighbourliness Convention, 1939 – are given in the second part.

149 **Tax havens of the world.**
Walter H. Diamond, Dorothy B. Diamond. New York: Matthew Bender, 1982. 3 vols.

Volume three of this work contains a short section on San Marino. There are short paragraphs on a range of topics including tax exemptions and reductions, investment and capital incentives, banking and foreign exchange, company information, entry into the state Registry of Enterprises, and details about the tax treaty with Italy. There is also some more general information about politics and communications links. It is pointed out that San Marino is not, in fact, a tax-free haven.

150 **Tax law and exchange control in the Republic of San Marino.**
Adriano Di Pietro. *Bulletin for International Fiscal Documentation,* vol. 37 (1983), no. 9-10, p. 438-40.

The tax system of San Marino is the result of successive fiscal provisions. Though influenced by the Italian fiscal system, there are notable differences in sectors like internal trade, real estate, and manufacturing. This article examines legislation on income tax (both normal and supplementary), indirect taxes (registration tax, estate tax, stamp tax and 'cinquina' tax), tax on imports, and minor taxes (e.g. on mortgages). References to the relevant Sanmarinese legislative sources are given. The special Convention of 1939 affirmed the principle of free movement of goods and persons between Italy and San Marino. There is, consequently, no regulation regarding movement of capital between San Marino and Italy, and between Italy and other states. Italian exchange control rules apply in the latter case.

Emilia Romagna.
See item no. 135.

Agriculture

151 **L'agricoltura: cenni sull'evoluzione dell'agricoltura sammarinese nell'ultimo secolo.** (Agriculture: an outline of the development of agriculture in San Marino in the last century.)
Marino Angelini. In: *Storia illustrata della Repubblica di San Marino*. San Marino: AIEP, 1985, p. 669-84. bibliog.

Up to the Second World War agriculture was the principal economic activity in San Marino. In 1908 some 71.4 per cent of the population were engaged in agricultural activity; by 1947 the figure was reduced to 40.7 per cent, and by 1974 to 8.5 per cent. This article examines the various attempts, during the first half of the century, at agricultural reform that would increase production and, at the same time, improve the condition of workers. Umberto Cannata, director of the journal *L'Agricoltura* and holder of the 'cattedra ambulante di agricoltura', was a keen advocate of cooperation between land-owners and workers, and instrumental in the reforms of the agricultural tenants' pact in 1921 – these were abolished when the Partito Fascista Sammarinese came to power two years later. In the immediate post-war period the socialist government attempted to improve the condition of agricultural workers and offer them more incentives but, after 1957, agriculture further declined as successive governments favoured industrial and tourist development. The article concludes with an analysis of the present state of Sammarinese agriculture and is supplemented by useful statistical charts.

152 **La cultura materiale: agricoltura ed archeologia rurale.** (Material culture: agriculture and rural archaeology.)
Giorgio Pedrocco. In: *Storia illustrata della Repubblica di San Marino*. San Marino: AIEP, 1985, p. 861-92. bibliog.

The author examines rural archaeology, a somewhat neglected area in San Marino studies, discussing rural houses, their architecture and their functional arrangements. He also examines, and illustrates, the furnishings and implements (by now virtually extinct) used in these houses. In the second part of the article he outlines the vicissitudes of agriculture and viticulture, for centuries the mainstays of San Marino's economy, and the relation between tradition and innovation.

Ambiente, insediamenti, agricoltura e industria fra XVIII e XX secolo: brevi note di storia economica sammarinese. (Environment, settlements, agriculture and industry from the eighteenth to the twentieth centuries: brief notes on San Marino's economic history.)
See item no. 133.

Statistics

153 **Statistics Europe: sources for social, economic and market research.**
Joan M. Harvey. Beckenham, England: CBD Research Ltd, 1987. 5th ed. 320p.

The section on San Marino on pages 259-60 gives the address of the Central Statistical Office and lists publications on: general statistics; agriculture; fisheries, forestry, etc; industry; construction; external trade; internal distribution and service trades; population; and finance.

154 **Statistics sources: a subject guide to data on industrial, business, social, educational, financial, and other topics for the United States and internationally.**
Edited by Jacqueline Wasserman O'Brien, Steven R. Wasserman. Detroit, Michigan: Gale Research, 1990. 13th ed. 2 vols.

This work is arranged by subject, but under the heading 'San Marino' (vol. 2, p. 2892-6) an indication can be found of where to track down statistics on subjects as varied as women in agricultural employment and school library facilities. All the references are to works emanating from the Food and Agriculture Organization, the World Health Organization or the Statistical Office of the United Nations.

Education

155 **Da centro a baricentro, prospettive della formazione professionale: un'indagine tra imprenditori e studenti nella Repubblica di San Marino.** (From centre to epicentre, opportunities for professional training: a survey carried out among entrepreneurs and students in the Republic of San Marino.)
Stefano Lombardini.   Milan, Italy: Franco Angeli, 1991. 141p.
(Collana di Sociologia, no. 188).

In this survey carried out in San Marino, twenty-five employers were asked questions relating to the education and training of their staff, such as which foreign languages are most useful in their company, and what links they have with training organizations. The companies varied in size, nature of business, use of technology and were from all corners of the Republic. One hundred and sixty-nine secondary school students were then questioned about their career aspirations, backgrounds, scholarly and free-time interests. The information gathered is assessed in Section three, and criteria for restructuring San Marino's Centro di Formazione Professionale (Centre for Professional Training) are identified. The questionnaires are included as appendixes to the volume.

156 **La scuola: note storiche sugli sviluppi dell' istruzione superiore.**
(Schools: historical notes on developments in secondary school teaching.)
Carla Nicolini, Filiberto Bernardi.   In: *Storia illustrata della Repubblica di San Marino.*   San Marino: AIEP, 1985, p. 781-96.
bibliog.

The existence of a school in San Marino is recorded in the Statutes of 1600, though mention of a preceptor goes back to 1468. This article gives an outline of the history of education in the Republic from 1468, the year in which the existence of a preceptor in the pay of the State is first recorded, to the development of teaching in the seventeenth century and the establishment of the secular Collegio Belluzzi in 1691 which was eventually to become the Liceo Ginnasio after the educational reforms of

Education

1883. Though the main object of these reforms was the recognition of San Marino educational qualifications in Italy, the bilateral agreement between the two countries was only signed exactly a century later and finally ratified in 1985. A chronology of the main stages leading to this agreement is given in a separate section. The article also includes a detailed description of the structure of the five-year programmes of the Scuola Media Superiore.

Organi istituzionali e amministrazione pubblica. (Institutional bodies and public administration.)
See item no. 119.

Literature

Works of Sanmarinese origin

157   **Giovanni Bertoldi da Serravalle tra i grandi cultori di Dante.**
(Giovanni Bertoldi da Serravalle and his place among the great Dante scholars.)
Teodosio Lombardi. *Studi Sammarinesi*, vol. 5 (1988), p. 17-42.

Giovanni Bertoldi (1355-1445), an early commentator on Dante, came from a San Marino Guelph family which had been driven into exile in Serravalle (then under the dominion of the Malatesta of Rimini) when the Ghibelline faction came to power in the Republic in 1253. This article, the result of extensive research in the archives of San Marino, Imola, Bologna and Perugia, gives an account of Bertoldi's scholastic formation, his teaching, his travels (which included a visit to Palestine and stays in Naples and England), and his participation in the Council of Constance. It was for the benefit of the foreign prelates attending this Council that Bertoldi translated Dante's *Divine Comedy* into Latin and wrote an accompanying commentary. This he achieved in less than a year. Extracts from the translation are compared with Matteo Ronto's contemporary translation of the poem. The author rejects Ugo Foscolo's unfavourable remarks about Bertoldi's translation and praises its vigour, simplicity and clarity. He also considers his commentary to be on the same level as those of Benvenuto Rambaldi da Imola and Giovanni Boccaccio. The article includes a bibliography of works on Bertoldi, together with extensive notes on other early Dante commentators.

158   **Letteratura dialettale sammarinese.** (Sanmarinese dialect literature.)
Giuseppe Macina. *Studi Sammarinesi*, vol. 5 (1988), p. 131-46.

This article begins with an assessment of how dialectal poetry in San Marino changed during the first half of this century. The first two decades showed a continuation of nineteenth-century content and style, with poets looking for answers to moral, political and social problems, but this changed in the 1930s. The work of two poets from this period is studied in detail: Nino Lombardi (1901-37), who was initially published under the name Italo Lombardi, and Marino Rossi (1886-1964). The author traces the development of style and content in their poetry, quoting several stanzas but few works in their entirety. The article contains bibliographical references.

Bibliografia delle tradizioni popolari di San Marino. (Bibliography of popular traditions in San Marino.)
See item no. 242.

Works about San Marino

159 **The patriot of San Marino.**
Grey Antony.   In: *The three stories of Grey Antony*.   London: Joseph Graham, 1845, p. 57-120.
This nineteenth-century English short story, set in 1507, relates how one young man organizes San Marino's fight against the threat of Venetian invasion. It contains one engraving depicting the hero in traditional costume.

160 **San Marino: poemetto in versi sciolti.** (San Marino: short poem in blank verse.)
Giovanni Chiaia.   *Libertas Perpetua: Museum*, year 4, no. 1 (Oct. 1935-April 1936), p. 11-35.
G. Chiaia (1799-1888), a native of Apulia in southern Italy, composed this ode to San Marino in 1871. An account of the poet's life and a study on the poem itself precede the text.

161 **Sant'Agata: dramma storico in un atto e tre quadri.** (Saint Agatha: a historical drama in one act and three scenes.)
Ugo Falena.   *Libertas Perpetua: Museum*, year 4, no. 2 (April-Oct. 1936), p. 6-60.
Based on the events of 1739-40, this work tells the story of Cardinal Alberoni's occupation of San Marino. It is as historically accurate as possible, and includes bibliographical notes. Colour drawings illustrate the playwright's suggestions for costumes and set designs.

Visual Arts

162 **L'arte: percorso nella scultura e pittura dal secolo XIV al primo Novecento.** (Art: an outline of sculpture and painting from the fourteenth to the early twentieth century.)
Laura Lazzarini. In: *Storia illustrata della Repubblica di San Marino.* San Marino: AIEP, 1985, p. 109-24.

Lazzarini traces the tradition of the stonecutters which goes back to St. Marinus. These artisans, whose identity remains obscure because of a lack of attributable works, were often in demand beyond the confines of San Marino. The tradition of stonecutting continues to the present century with the Reffi family which has provided a long line of sculptors and decorative artists. During the Renaissance San Marino produced only two notable artists. Antonio Orafo (ca. 1450-1522) was one of the great goldsmiths of his time. He worked both in Rome, for Julius II and Leo X, and at Urbino, where he was a friend and collaborator of Raphael. A number of works in San Marino are attributed to him. Giovan Battista Belluzzi (1506-54), called 'Il Sammarino', was a military architect, a writer (he wrote a treatise on fortifications and an autobiographical diary in which he describes his formative years and travels), and a diplomat. The only notable Sanmarinese painters were Pietro Tonnini (1820-94), an Academic artist, and Federico Martelli, called 'Bico' (1900-72), whose output ranges from religious works and portraits to caricatures and scenes of contemporary life. He was also a noted draughtsman and restorer of works of art in the Museum of San Marino. The article is accompanied by a number of illustrations of the works of these artists.

163 **L'arte dal dopoguerra in poi: itinerari dei contemporanei a San Marino.** (Art from 1945 to date: itineraries of contemporary artists in San Marino).
Leonardo Casadei. In: *Storia illustrata della Repubblica di San Marino.* San Marino: AIEP, 1985, p. 798-812. bibliog.

In the years before the Second World War, artistic creativity in San Marino remained largely closed to avant-garde trends and limited to post-Impressionist or nationalist works. After 1945 the Republic became more open to external influences, especially those of major Italian artistic centres, such as Bologna, Milan, Turin and Rome. Manifestations like the Premio d'Arte Figurativa del Titano (1956), the Biennale per la Pittura (1959-67) and the annual Rassegna d'Arte 'Castello di Serravalle' (1963-82), as well as major exhibitions of the work of well-known artists, aimed to increase awareness of international artistic trends but also attract tourism to San Marino. The first nucleus of a state collection of modern art was formed in 1974 and led to the creation of the Galleria Nazionale d'Arte Moderna, itself the organizer of important exhibitions of contemporary art. This article, which examines in detail these developments, contains a number of colour and black-and-white illustrations of works exhibited in San Marino.

164 **La bottega dei Coda e il polittico di Valdragone.** (The Coda workshop and the Valdragone polyptych.)
Edited by Pier Giorgio Pasini. San Marino: Museo di Stato, 1988. 114p. bibliog. (Mostre del Museo di Stato, no. 5).

This exhibition catalogue gives a history of the Coda family, who were working in Rimini in the sixteenth century, followed by chapters on the restoration of one of the more important surviving works, the polyptych at the Monastero di Santa Maria dei Servi in Valdragone.

165 **La pittura a San Marino.** (Painting in San Marino.)
Corrado Ricci. *Rassegna d'Arte*, year 1, no. 9 (Sept. 1901), p. 129-32.

This is a brief look at some of the paintings housed in the Republic's churches. All the works considered are by Italian artists, as the author states that San Marino has only ever produced one artist of note, the military architect Giovan Battista Belluzzi. Two illustrations support the text – both images of the Madonna with saints by Girolamo Marchesi di Cotignola (ca.1481-ca.1550).

166 **La Repubblica di San Marino.** (The Republic of San Marino.)
Corrado Ricci. Bergamo, Italy: Istituto Italiano d'Arti Grafiche, 1928. 108p. (Collezione di Monografie Illustrate, Serie Italia Artistica, no. 5).

A well-illustrated artistic history of San Marino from earliest times to the nineteenth century, with an emphasis on buildings in the capital and art works then found in the State Museum. Although chiefly concerned with the city of San Marino, there are brief entries on other locations such as Serravalle and Faetano.

167 **Scoperte e studi su Genga pittore.** (Discoveries and studies on the painter Genga.)
Walter Fontana. Urbino, Italy: Accademia Raffaello, 1981. 115p.

Fontana attributes a number of works to the Urbinate painter Girolamo Genga. These include a polyptych with the Holy Family in the Pinacoteca dello Stato. The polyptych, which in the past was attributed to Giulio Romano, is the most important painting in San Marino. The central panel suffered damage in the bombing of June 1944.

Guida storica-artistica illustrata della Repubblica di San Marino. (Illustrated historical and artistic guide to the Republic of San Marino.)
See item no. 44.

Gli istituti culturali: il Museo di Stato. (Cultural institutions: the State Museum.)
See item no. 223.

Stamps and Coins

Stamps

168　**Bolaffi Sassone catalogo blu 1995.** (Bolaffi Sassone blue catalogue.)
　　　Turin, Italy: Giulio Bolaffi, 1994. 336p.

Published as a supplement to the philatelic journal *Il Collezionista Francobolli* (July-Aug. 1994 issue), this is a catalogue of postage stamps from Italy and the former Italian states, the Vatican, San Marino, the Sovereign Military Order of Malta and the internal issues of the company Plurinvest. San Marino issues 1877 to May 1994 are arranged chronologically on pages 218-83. Colour illustrations accompany most entries, and a dealer's price is given for mint and used examples. There are appendices of airmail stamps, souvenir sheets, express, parcel and postage due stamps.

169　**Catalogo enciclopedico italiano.** (Italian encyclopaedic catalogue.)
　　　Milan, Italy: Augusto Ferrara, 1987- . 2 vols. annual.

This work contains, in volume one, a comprehensive catalogue of San Marino postage stamps and franking marks from 1862 to the present day. General postage issues are arranged in chronological order, each is illustrated in black and white, and the dealer's price for mint and used examples is quoted. A price is also given for stamps still attached to the envelope. There are appendices of commemorative and first day of issue envelopes, booklets, souvenir sheets, airmail stamps and aerogrammes, express, parcel and postage due stamps.

170　**Francobolli: linee di storia postale e filatelica.** (Postage stamps: an
　　　outline of postal and philatelic history.)
　　　Giuseppe Morganti.　In: *Storia illustrata della Repubblica di San
　　　Marino.*　San Marino: AIEP, 1985, p. 829-44.

San Marino has one of the oldest postal services in the world, its origins going back to 1607 when a postman was appointed by the state to deliver letters to and from Rimini. This article looks at some key dates in the development of the service, such as the establishment of the first post office in 1833, the first Postal Convention between Italy and San Marino (1865) which allowed the Republic to use Italian stamps, and the first issue of San Marino stamps (1877). It also examines the development of philately and the subject-matter of various commemorative issues which include the inauguration of the Palazzo del Governo in 1894, views of Monte Titano, the Rimini–San Marino railway, Garibaldi and Abraham Lincoln.

171 **Le poste di Romagna.** (The postal services of Romagna.)
     Francesco Mainoldi.   Bologna, Italy: Guidicini e Rosa, 1981. 138p.
     map.

An account of postal services in San Marino and the Italian towns of Forlì, Cesena and Rimini from the sixteenth century to 1890. It includes a well-illustrated catalogue of postmarks.

172 **Stanley Gibbons stamp catalogue. Part 8: Italy and Switzerland.**
     London: Stanley Gibbons, 1983. 2nd ed. 269p.

The complete catalogue of San Marino's philatelic output from 1877 to 1982 is covered on pages 151-83. The issues are arranged chronologically, and include the dealer's sale prices for mint and used examples of each stamp. Most issues are illustrated with black-and-white photographs.

Coins

173 **Corpus nummorum italicorum: primo tentativo di un catalogo generale delle monete medievali e moderne coniate in Italia o da italiani in altri paesi.** (Corpus nummorum italicorum : first draft of a general catalogue of medieval and modern coins minted in Italy or by Italians in other countries.)
     Rome: Ludovico Cecchini, 1910-[43?]. 20 vols.

This major work is a description of the personal collection of King Umberto II of Italy, a keen numismatist. Volume X, the second of the two tomes dealing with Emilia, contains a catalogue of San Marino coins 1864-1925 on pages 725-9. Each is described in detail, with the exact style of lettering reproduced, and is illustrated on plate xlviii. There are occasional references to other collections which were known to contain examples of each coin.

174 **Esperienze sulla monetazione sammarinese.** (Experiments in San Marino coinage.)
     Giuseppe Rossi.   *Studi Sammarinesi*, vol. 1 (1984), p. 159-83.

This article is essentially a chronological history of San Marino coinage. Every issue from 1972 to 1983 is described and background information provided. There are photographs of the obverse and reverse of each one.

175 **La moneta metallica in Italia.** (Metallic coins in Italy.)
Edited by Nicola Jelpo.   Rome: Istituto Poligrafico e Zecca dello
Stato, 1980. 141p.

This work is principally concerned with the history of minting and control of coinage
in Italy and surrounding areas. The short piece on San Marino (p. 72-3) gives brief
details about the 1897 agreement with Italy that allowed the Republic to issue its own
coinage, provided that it was minted exclusively by the Italian State Mint. Details are
also given about the agreement of 1971 whereby San Marino again began to issue its
own coins after a break of around thiry-two years. The piece ends with a description
of the first gold currency issue of 1974.

176 **Monete italiane dall'invasione napoleonica ai giorni nostri,
1796-1961.** (Italian coins from the Napoleonic invasion to the present
day, 1796-1961.)
Antonio Pagani.   Milan, Italy: Mario Ratto, 1962. 363p. bibliog.

From 1864 to 1938-39 San Marino issued its own coinage for the first time. On pages
169-72 of this volume, there is a very brief introduction and a catalogue of forty-four
coins from this period, arranged by face values. The obverse and reverse of each is
described, and there is an assessment of its rarity. Eleven are also illustrated.

177 **Nove monete per San Marino.** (Nine coins for San Marino.)
Milan, Italy: All'Insegna del Pesce d'Oro, 1976. [39]p. (Quaderni
d'Arte del Pesce d'Oro, no. 19).

This booklet illustrates and describes the 1976 special issue of nine commemorative
coins, with an introductory essay by the artist M. Molteni.

178 **Segni d'onore e distintivi del Regno d'Italia e degli ex stati italiani.**
(Marks of honour and distinction of the Kingdom of Italy and the
former Italian states.)
H. von Heyden.   Wiesbaden, Germany: Keyssner'sche
Hofbuchdruckerei, 1910. 451p.

This work looks at medals awarded for bravery, merit and old age by the Kingdom of
Italy, the Kingdom of the Two Sicilies, the Papal States, the Holy See and the
Republic of San Marino. On pages 307-11, there are details of five sets of awards
made by San Marino between 1823 and 1875. Each of the medals (gold, silver,
bronze, etc.) is described and information given about the artist and the reason for the
award. The obverse and reverse of each is illustrated in the plates at the end of the
volume. The text is in German and Italian.

179 **Super manuale del collezionista di monete decimali italiane, con valutazioni, numero dei pezzi coniati e ritirati dal 1798 al 1976.**
(Super manual for the collector of Italian decimal coins, with valuations, numbers minted and withdrawn from 1798 to 1976.)
Cesare Bobba. Asti, Italy: The author, 1975. 368p.

A catalogue of San Marino coinage is to be found on pages 282-90. Coins issued by the Republic from 1864 to 1938-39 and in the early 1970s are included, being arranged by face value. Each is illustrated and described, with an assessment of its rarity. The place of minting is given, and shows that not all coins were produced in Rome; some were struck in Milan. The section ends with the two gold pieces and the eight general-circulation coins depicting wildlife which were produced in 1974.

Architecture and Town Planning

180 **L'architettura: la casa.** (Architecture: houses.)
Leo Marino Morganti. In: *Storia illustrata della Repubblica di San Marino*. San Marino: AIEP, 1985, p. 157-72. bibliog.

This article is the first in a series looking at buildings in San Marino, this part being a survey of houses and related building types. It begins with a brief look at Bronze Age and Roman dwellings, and goes on to describe medieval and later buildings in greater detail, with sections on the palaces of the nobility, monasteries (especially the Convento di Santa Chiara), forts, mills, dovecotes, and rural dwellings (especially those of rural landlords). The article concludes with a consideration of housing in the twentieth century. It contains a large number of photographs, plans, elevations and two bibliographies.

181 **L'architettura: il Convento di Santa Chiara nella città antica.**
(Architecture: the Convent of Saint Clare in the old town.)
Marino Morganti. In: *Storia illustrata della Repubblica di San Marino*. San Marino: AIEP, 1985, p. 813-28. bibliog.

The Convent of Saint Clare was founded in 1609; its building began some forty-four years earlier at the instigation of Costantino Bonelli, the bishop of Città del Castello but was interrupted in 1572 because of lack of funds. It was finally completed in 1609 largely thanks to a donation by Vincenza Lunardini, who became one of the first Clares of the convent. In 1968 the State purchased the convent and, after the nuns moved to Valdragone (Borgo Maggiore), work began on its restoration for re-use as a cultural centre. As well as the history of the convent, this article examines its architecture and its relation to the historic centre of San Marino. It includes various plans and photographs.

182   **Case contadine.** (Rural houses.)
Texts by Giacomo Corna Pellegrini (et al.).   Milan, Italy: Touring
Club Italiano, 1979. 208p. (Italia Meravigliosa).

The contribution by Massimo Quaini on houses of the central and northern Apennines
(p. 92-105) deals with the types of buildings found in San Marino. The black-and-
white photographs depict not only the vernacular architecture, but also rural mountain
life in this part of the Italian peninsula during the first half of this century.

183   **La Chiesa Vecchia di San Marino.** (The Old Church of San Marino.)
Gino Zani.   *Libertas Perpetua: Museum*, year 3, no. 1 (Oct. 1934-
April 1935), p. 74-105.

This well-illustrated article describes the old parish church of the city of San Marino,
first recorded in 1113, and traces its history. The building was demolished in 1825 to
make way for a new church of neoclassical design.

184   **Due proposte di convivenza del progettista sammarinese Gilberto
Rossini.** (Two community projects by the San Marino architect
Gilberto Rossini.)
Renato Pedio.   *L'Architettura, Cronache e Storia*, vol. 30, no. 12,
issue 350 (Dec. 1984), p. 860-7.

In this article, Pedio looks at two buildings: the nursery school in the Ca' Ragni area
of Dogana and a family house at Murata, both designed by the San Marino architect
Gilberto Rossini. The article largely consists of photographs, plans and sections. There
is a brief English summary of the Italian text on page 862.

185   **Edificio per attività di interesse pubblico nella Repubblica di San
Marino.** (New civic facilities for the Republic of San Marino.)
Sergio Petruccioli.   *Industria delle Costruzioni*, vol. 25, no. 236
(June 1991), p. 4-11.

This article looks at the new multi-purpose civic centre located in the city of San
Marino. The complex, which incorporates stairs and lifts between different levels of
the city, a meeting hall, administrative offices, shops and cafés was designed by
Franco Cervellini and Sergio Petruccioli (the author of this piece), together with the
practice Gregotti Associati. The article contains photographs, plans, sections and
elevations; the text is in Italian and English.

186   **Edilizia pubblica residenziale a San Marino.** (Housing in San
Marino.)
Fiamma Dinelli.   *Industria delle Costruzioni*, vol. 14, no. 100, issue 2
(Feb. 1980), p. 13-20.

This article looks at a public housing project in Faetano, completed in 1977. The
architect was Franco Cervellini, with assistance from Roberto Perris. The text is in
Italian and English, and is illustrated with photographs, plans, sections and elevations.

187 **Le fortificazioni del Monte Titano.** (The fortifications of Mount Titano.)
Gino Zani. Naples, Italy: Istituto Arti Grafiche G. Rispoli, 1933. 183p.

The author, Gino Zani, was responsible for restoring the fortifications and monuments of the city of San Marino during the 1920s. In this volume, he describes the capital's walls, towers and castles and provides the historical context for their construction. The fortifications were mostly designed by the sixteenth-century military architect Giovan Battista Belluzzi, and his life and work are examined in detail. The text is accompanied by a large number of illustrations and plans.

188 **Gilberto Rossini: impianti collettivi come paesaggio urbano.** (Gilberto Rossini: community establishments as urban landscape.)
Giovanni Michelucci. *L'Architettura, Cronache e Storia*, vol. 28, no. 5, issue 319 (May 1982), p. 318-27.

Two buildings by San Marino-born architect Gilberto Rossini are looked at in this article: the primary school at Murata and the community centre at Fiorentino. There are plans, sections and photographs of the buildings, and an English summary on page 318.

189 **Gino Zani: la rifabbrica di San Marino, 1925-1943.** (Gino Zani: the rebuilding of San Marino, 1925-43.)
Guido Zucconi. Venice, Italy: Arsenale, 1992. 93p. (Architettura, no. 4).

In 1925 Gino Zani was charged with restoring the heart of the city of San Marino. This book examines his work, looking at the public buildings, churches, fortifications and other monuments that he was responsible for restoring. There are many illustrations, including contemporary photographs, plans, portraits and facsimiles of documents.

190 **Il gioco della continuità.** (The continuity game.)
Gilberto Rossini. *L'Architettura, Cronache e Storia*, vol. 39, no. 12, issue 458 (Dec. 1993), p. 838-47.

Two public buildings designed by Gilberto Rossini are dealt with in this article: the Asilo nido or nursery school at Cailungo, and an enclosed shooting range at Ca' Martino (Acquaviva). The piece consists chiefly of photographs, plans and sections, but there is also a small amount of text which is translated into English.

191 **Giovan Battista Belluzzi.**
M. Antonietta Bonelli. In: *Storia illustrata della Repubblica di San Marino*. San Marino: AIEP, 1985, p. 173-88. bibliog.

G. B. Belluzzi, 1506-54, came from a Sanmarinese noble family and became one of the most eminent military architects of sixteenth-century Italy. This article looks at Belluzzi's civic and military designs, and his life, of which much is known as a diary for 1535-41 has been preserved. The story of Belluzzi's death, which occurred in Tuscany whilst working for Duke Cosimo I, is surrounded by mystery and the author attempts to determine the facts of his death. The text is accompanied by illustrations taken largely from Belluzzi's treatise *Il Trattato delle fortificazioni*, and by a letter written in his own hand, now in the State Archive.

192 **Giovanni Michelucci: il pensiero e le opere.** (Giovanni Michelucci: his thought and his work.)
University of Bologna Institute of Architecture and Urban Studies.
Bologna, Italy: Pàtron, 1966. 242p. bibliog.

G. Michelucci was one of Italy's most eminent twentieth-century architects. In 1961 he designed the small church at Borgo Maggiore, which is today seen as one of San Marino's most important pieces of modern architecture. This volume looks at most of G. Michelucci's works to 1966, with descriptions, plans, photographs and sketches of the Borgo Maggiore church on pages 178-93.

193 **Una piscina a San Marino.** (A swimming pool in San Marino.)
L'Architettura, Cronache e Storia, vol. 25, no. 5, issue 284
(June 1979), p. 336-9.

San Marino's only indoor public swimming baths were opened in 1979. The building was designed by the Sanmarinese architect Gilberto Rossini. This article includes photographs, plans and sections of the buildings, as well as some text. An English summary is to be found on page 337.

194 **Recupero di una casa colonica a San Marino.** (Renovation of a farm house in San Marino.)
Ville Giardini, no. 127 (Oct. 1978), p. 26-9.

This article which consists chiefly of plans and colour photographs, looks at the restoration of a large rural house somewhere in the Republic of San Marino. The emphasis is on the interior design aspects.

195 **Residenza a Falciano, San Marino.** (A family house at Falciano, San Marino.)
Giancarlo Priori. *Industria delle Costruzioni*, vol. 22, no. 200
(June 1988), p. 32-7.

The Reggini residence at Falciano was designed by the Italian architect Claudio D'Amato. This article examines this hillside villa, and includes photographs, plans, sections, elevations and architect's sketches. The text is in both Italian and English.

196 **Scuola elementare di Ca' Caccio, San Marino.** (A primary school at Ca' Caccio, San Marino.)
Giovanni Michelucci. *L'Architettura, Cronache e Storia*, vol. 18,
no. 9, issue 207 (Jan. 1973), p. 567-75.

This article chiefly consists of black-and-white photographs of the school designed by Gilberto Rossini in via Ca' Caccio, San Marino city. It contains a small amount of biographical material about the architect, who was born and works in San Marino.

197 **Scuola elementare e materna a San Marino.** (A primary and nursery school in San Marino.)
Renato Pedio. *L'Architettura, Cronache e Storia*, vol. 36, no. 3, issue 413 (March 1990), p. 166-74.
The combined nursery and primary school at Cailungo was designed by San Marino architect Gilberto Rossini. This article examines the building, which is focused on a central piazza, and includes photographs, plans, sections and elevations. The text is in Italian, but there are summaries in English, French, German and Spanish on page 168.

198 **Scuola elementare, San Marino.** (A primary school, San Marino.)
L'Architettura, Cronache e Storia, vol. 37, no. 6, issue 428 (June 1991), p. 520-3.
The primary school in question is that at Ca' Ragni (Dogana), which the article 'Due proposte di convivenza del progettista sammarinese Gilberto Rossini' cited in item no. 184 also examined. The construction is now complete and the school is in use. This article revisits the complex, and includes a new set of photographs, plans and sections.

199 **Teatro-cinema a San Marino.** (Theatre/cinema in San Marino.)
L'Architettura, Storia e Cronache, vol. 20, no. 5, issue 227 (Sept. 1974), p. 286-95.
Designed by Gilberto Rossini, this open-air theatre space and indoor auditorium was opened in San Marino city in 1974. The article chiefly consists of photographs, plans, sections and elevations, with some text which is summarized in English on page 286.

200 **Traditional houses of rural Italy.**
Paul Duncan. London: Collins & Brown, 1993. 159p.
This lavishly illustrated work examines the vernacular architecture of northern Italy. The chapter on Emilia-Romagna (p. 94-113) contains many examples of the types found in San Marino, with colour photographs of structures and architectural details.

201 **La trasformazione del territorio.** (The transformation of the land.)
Gilberto Rossini. In: *Storia illustrata della Repubblica di San Marino.* San Marino: AIEP, 1985, p. 621-52.
Covering the period 1945 to 1981, this article describes the recording and planning of San Marino's built environment, from roads to settlements. It looks at changes in planning policy, at the increasing urbanization of the Republic during the 1960s, and at attempts to rationalize the Piano Regolatore Generale (general planning scheme) in 1981. The article contains statistics from the 1947 population census, land-use figures from 1985, and the state budgets 1945-81. It contains a large number of maps, plans and photographs.

202 **La trasformazione della forma urbana.** (Transformation of the urban environment.)
Gilberto Rossini.   In: *Storia illustrata della Repubblica di San Marino*.   San Marino: AIEP, 1985, p. 573-620.

Beginning in the fifteenth century, this article looks at town planning, architecture and construction in the city of San Marino. Major sections deal with the eighteenth century, the Fascist period, and the recent decline in the residential use of the city centre. It contains a large number of photographs, plans and drawings.

Folklore and Customs

Folklore and oral tradition

203 **Fiabe romagnole e emiliane.** (Emilian and Romagnol fables.)
Edited by Elide Casali. Milan, Italy: Mondadori, 1986. 213p. bibliog.
(Oscar Narrativa, no. 792).

This is a collection of thirty-four fables translated into modern standard Italian. They come from all over the cultural area of Emilia and Romagna, which incorporates San Marino, although none are recorded as specifically originating there. The introduction and notes give a wider Italian and European context to the stories.

204 **Letteratura popolare sammarinese.** (San Marino popular literature.)
Giuseppe Macina. *Studi Sammarinesi*, vol. 6 (1989), p. 101-18.

This work is divided in two. The first part looks at traditional stories, giving an overview, examining content and style, and considering how the same story was told in different ways by different storytellers. Much of this section concentrates on the life and work of Walter Anderson who collected large numbers of stories, principally from school children, during his visits to the Republic in the 1920s and early 1930s. The second part looks at legends. Again, general characteristics and themes are described and the story of Saint Marinus is examined in detail.

205 **Novelline popolari sammarinesi.** (Popular San Marino stories.)
Edited by Walter Anderson. Turin, Italy: Bottega D'Erasmo, 1960.
1 vol.

This title is a reprint of papers originally published in Tartu (Estonia), in series B of the *Acta et Commentationes Universitatis Tartuensis* in the volumes for 1927, 1929 and 1933. Anderson supervised the recording of 118 stories as told by school children in San Marino primary schools: some in Italian, some in dialect. The text includes notes and bibliographical references.

206   **Repertorio della narrativa popolare romagnola.** (A collection of
      popular Romagnol stories.)
      Stefano Orioli.   Florence, Italy: Olschki, 1984. 143p. map. (Studi
      [dell'] Accademia Toscana di Scienze e Lettere La Colombaria,
      no. 68).

This bibliography of folk tales from Romagna contains several stories from San
Marino recorded not just in the capital, but also in Serravalle, Acquaviva, Faetano,
Montegiardino and Chiesanuova. The entries are collected under the headings 'fables',
'stories', 'legends' and 'short stories', and then subdivided by subject. The
introductory essay traces the development of oral tradition recording in the area.

Folk music and dance

207   **La cultura popolare.** (Popular culture.)
      Giuseppe Pelliconi.   In: *Storia illustrata della Repubblica di San
      Marino.*   San Marino: AIEP, 1985, p. 845-60. bibliog.

Although it shares many elements with the customs and traditions of Romagna and
Montefeltro, Sanmarinese folklore has its own characteristics. This article looks at
folklore in its various manifestations, including local customs and traditions, ritual
feasts, superstitions, and food. In particular, it examines the cycle of seasonal feasts
and customs related to the Church and solar calendar, legends related to the history of
the Republic (e.g. about Saint Marinus, Cardinal Alberoni, Napoleon, Garibaldi) or
explaining its toponymy. It also looks at popular literature, in particular the work of
Pietro Rossi (1804-79) whose poetry reflects the popular ideology of his time, and of
Nino Lombardi (1901-87).

208   **Folclorismo musicale sammarinese.** (Sanmarinese musical folklore.)
      Celio Gozi.   *Libertas Perpetua: Museum*, year 6, no. 2 (April-Oct.
      1938), p. 123-36.

This article begins by looking at popular dancing in the 1930s. It goes on to list and
describe the local parish 'sagre' in the Republic, giving the texts of several traditional
songs recorded at these festivals.

209   **E saltarel sammarines.** (The Sanmarinese saltarello.)
      Celio Gozi.   *Libertas Perpetua: Museum*, year 5, no. 1 (Oct. 1936-
      April 1937), p. 133-9.

The saltarello was a traditional dance still performed at country festivals in the 1930s.
This article describes the structure of the music, the instruments used and the dance
steps. Three drawings by the author accompany the text.

210   **Vi do la buonasera: studi sul canto popolare in Romagna, il**
      repertorio lirico. (I bid you good afternoon: studies on popular songs
      in Romagna, the lyrical repertory.)
      Tullia Magrini, Giuseppe Bellosi.   Bologna, Italy: CLUEB, 1982.
      286p. bibliog.

This work examines folk songs from the cultural area of Romagna from a technical
point of view, concentrating more on the musical formulae than on the words. 'Vi do
la buonasera' is the title of one of the songs studied.

Festivals

211   **La festa nel folclore sammarinese.** (Festivals in San Marino
      folklore.)
      Giuseppe Macina.   *Studi Sammarinesi*, vol. 5 (1988), p. 147-68.

Macina's article is divided into three parts. The first examines religious holidays. The
way in which Christmas, Epiphany and Easter were traditionally celebrated is
described with quotations of dialectal poetry and popular sayings. Saints' days,
especially those of Saint Joseph and the Virgin Mary, were times of celebration
involving fire, and the author studies the interpretations of other scholars. The second
part looks at how the Sanmarinese celebrated holidays such as Carnival
('Carnevalone' - the first Sunday in Lent – being especially important) and May Day.
The last part examines the ways in which people enjoyed themselves on their days off,
concentrating on singing, dancing and game playing. The article is accompanied by a
large number of bibliographical references.

212   **La tradizionale Festa del Santo Fondatore e la Sagra del Littorio**
      sammarinese. (The traditional festival of the Holy Founder and the
      Feast of the San Marino Fascist Party.)
      Federico Gozi.   *Libertas Perpetua: Museum*, year 2, no. 2
      (April-Oct. 1934), p. 174-81.

During the Fascist period in the Italian peninsula, traditional festivals were revived
and often linked with 'sagre', public open-air festivals, usually financed by the Party.
San Marino's Festival of the Holy Founder was one such event, celebrated at the
beginning of September. This article describes the festival of 1934, and includes two
photographs.

Customs

213 **Riti del nascere: gravidanza, parto e battesimo nella cultura popolare romagnola.** (Birth customs: pregnancy, childbirth and baptism in Romagnol popular culture.)
Eraldo Baldini. Ravenna, Italy: Longo, 1991. 166p. bibliog. (Mondo Popolare, no. 3).

This work documents popular beliefs and aspirations about conception, pregnancy, the desire for male children, birth, baptism and babies throughout the cultural area of Romagna, which includes San Marino. The text is well supported by bibliographical references.

Food and Drink

214 **The food and drink of Italy.**
Claudia Roden. London: Chatto & Windus, 1989. 218p.
Despite there being many general Italian cookery books available in English, there are
few that concentrate on any one geographical area. Those that exist deal mostly with
Sicilian or Tuscan cuisine. This volume by a well-known television cook covers the
whole of Italy, but is arranged by region. The section on the food of Emilia-Romagna
is on pages 75-91. There is a lengthy introduction, describing the characteristics of the
local cuisine, which is followed by around twenty typical recipes.

215 **Grande dizionario e ricettario gastronomico romagnolo.** (Great
dictionary and recipe book of Romagnol gastronomy.)
Gianni Quondamatteo. Imola, Italy: Grafiche Galeati, 1978. 350p.
The first part of this work is a twenty-eight-page Romagnol–Italian dictionary of
words connected with food and drink. This is followed by a much more substantial
Italian–Romagnol dictionary of culinary terms, which gives local variants and
examples of usage. Many entries include quotations, poems or essays relating to the
concept described. Quondamatteo has also inserted several longer culinary essays by
local writers which are separate from the A–Z sequence. The third part of the work
contains historical photographs of food, cooking, kitchens and kitchen equipment. The
work concludes with a collection of some seventy recipes from around Romagna.

Sports and Recreation

216 **Lo sport.** (Sport.)
Marino Ercolani Casadei.   In: *Storia illustrata della Repubblica di San Marino*.   San Marino: AIEP, 1985, p. 893-924.

Gives San Marino's achievements in some twenty-six different sports, listed alphabetically, with brief accounts of the origins and development of each sport in the Republic.

Libraries, Art Galleries, Museums and Archives

217 **L'Archivio pubblico della Repubblica di San Marino.** (The Public Archive of the Republic of San Marino.)
Elisabetta Righi Iwanejko.   In: *Storia illustrata della Repubblica di San Marino*.   San Marino: AIEP, 1985, p. 733-48. bibliog.

Iwanejko explains the classification system of the Archive. It was developed by Carlo Malagola between 1885 and 1891 when he re-ordered the material into two distinct sections, the Archivio Governativo (Government Archive) and the Archivio Notarile (Notarial Archive). The arrangement of the former reflects the constitutional bodies of the Republic, while the latter contains notarial documents as well as papers related to the administration of the Archive. The article also describes the development of the Archive and enumerates its various inventories.

218 **La biblioteca di Giuliano Corbelli, giurista e politico sammarinese, 1515-1602.** (The library of Giuliano Corbelli, jurist and statesman of San Marino, 1515-1602.)
Laura Rossi.   [San Marino]: Cassa di Risparmio della Repubblica di San Marino, 1988. 193p. bibliog.

A well-documented biography of Giuliano Corbelli which includes a bibliography of 160 printed books. These formed his library, and were collected for their usefulness to his work as a politician. They are now in the State Library.

219 **L'epistolario di Matteo Valli nell'Archivio sammarinese.** (The correspondence of Matteo Valli in the San Marino Archive.)
Cristoforo Buscarini.   *Studi Sammarinesi*, vol. 1 (1984), p. 61-86.

Matteo Valli (1596-1657) held various diplomatic and governmental positions in San Marino, including Chancellor of the Republic and Judicial Chancellor. The early seventeenth century was an interesting period as control of San Marino passed from the Dukes of Urbino to the Holy See, and Valli was required to spend much of his time at the courts of the local dukes and bishops, representing the Republic's interests. This article examines chronologically the collection of official and personal letters that he sent from Casteldurante, Pesaro, Rome, Rimini and elsewhere, a collection which is now in the State Archive. The last part of the article consists of a description of *Dell'origine della Repubblica di San Marino*, a pamphlet written by Valli and printed by Giulio Crivellari in Padua in 1633.

220 **La fucina del professore: gli scritti, i manoscritti, l'archivio e la biblioteca di Pietro Franciosi.** (The forge of the professor: the writings, manuscripts, archive and library of Pietro Franciosi.) Edited by Gabriella Lorenzi, Silva Savoretti. San Marino: AIEP, 1986. 365p. (Biblioteca e Ricerca. Quaderni del Dicastero Pubblica Istruzione e Cultura, no. 3).

An inventory of the Pietro Franciosi's archive in the State Library of San Marino. There are separate listings of the manuscripts of his works, the contents of his personal archive, his correspondence and, finally, his library.

221 **Interventi di ristrutturazione su 'Palazzo Valloni' per una nuova articolazione degli spazi della Biblioteca di Stato.** (Notes on restructuring 'Palazzo Valloni': proposing new uses for space at the State Library.) Gilberto Rossini. In: *Biblioteca e Ricerca*. San Marino: AIEP, 1983, p. 43-5. (Quaderni del Dicastero Pubblica Istruzione e Cultura, no. 2).

Palazzo Valloni was home not just to the State Library, but also to the State Archive, the Art Gallery and the Archaeological Museum; and it included diplomatic reception rooms. By the 1980s the Library was experiencing serious problems with space and so the State Technical Office undertook a programme of restoration and refurbishment. This article outlines the alterations, and contains photographs and a plan of the ground floor.

222 **Gli istituti culturali: la Biblioteca di Stato.** (Cultural institutions: the State Library.) Elisabetta Righi Iwanejko. In: *Storia illustrata della Repubblica di San Marino*. San Marino: AIEP, 1985, p. 749-64.

The State Library first opened to the public in 1858 but the core of its collections was formed in 1839 through the purchase of the Onofri library and the acquisition, in 1840, of Palazzo Valloni and its book collection. By 1890 when a first catalogue of its holdings was compiled by Marino Borbicone and Pietro Franciosi, the Library had around 12,000 items. The collections were further enriched by some important donations at the beginning of this century, when some 25,000 items were added. The building suffered grave damage in 1944 due to Allied action and a number of precious items perished. In 1983 the Library became autonomous from the State Museum and, at the same time, it was reorganized and discrete areas of its collections, such as the Sanmarinese music and periodical publications, were re-ordered. Its role as a service to readers rather than as a museum of the book was emphasized through the creation of new reading areas and the development of an active education service. This has proved beneficial not only to the community but also to the Library itself, as in the case of the cataloguing of its collection of sixteenth-century books by library students of the Liceo Classico.

223 **Gli istituti culturali: il Museo di Stato.** (Cultural institutions: the
State Museum.)
Pier Giorgio Pasini. In: *Storia illustrata della Repubblica di San
Marino.* San Marino: AIEP, 1985, p. 765-80. bibliog.

The formation of the State Museum was due to the enthusiasm of Luigi Ciprario
(1802-70), the Piedmontese historian and man of letters. Largely through Ciprario's
influence, the Museum received a number of donations and when it finally opened to
the public, in 1899, its collections included paintings, coins and medals, Greek and
Roman vases, maps, stamps and Garibaldi memorabilia, all displayed together in
picturesque confusion. It was only after 1937 that its various components were
displayed separately and due prominence was given to the paintings collection (which
includes works by Guercino, Bernardo Strozzi and Pompeo Batoni) and those of
stamps and coins. The Museum suffered grave damage in 1944 and in the 1960s its
entire collection of coins and medals was stolen. In 1983 the Museum became
autonomous from the State Library and its collections were transferred from Palazzo
Valloni (which had previously housed both institutions) to Palazzo Pergami. The
article is well illustrated by some of the most important works (mostly paintings) in
the collection, including the nine panels of the polyptych elsewhere attributed to
Giulio Romano, Girolamo da Carpi or Girolamo Genga and here given to Francesco
Menzocchi.

224 **Serie documenti dell'Archivio di Stato di San Marino.** (Series of
documents from the State Archive of San Marino.)
Adele Bellù. In: *Le Signorie dei Malatesti: atti [di] una giornata di
studi malatestiani a San Marino.* Rimini, Italy: Bruno Ghigi, 1990,
p. 55-98. (Atti delle Giornate di Studi Malatestiani, no. 18).

In the Archivio Governativo della Repubblica di San Marino under the heading
'Registro di lettere', there is a collection of fourteenth- and fifteenth-century Latin and
Italian documents on subjects including military and political events, commerce and
justice. This paper, presented at a conference on Malatesta studies, places them in
context and reproduces their texts.

225 **Tre icone inedite del Museo di Stato di San Marino.** (Three
unknown icons in the State Museum of San Marino.)
Silvia Pasi. *Studi Sammarinesi*, vol. 6 (1989), p. 119-29.

All three icons belong to the Veneto-Cretan school of painting, which adapted
Byzantine stylistic and iconographic elements to Western figurative schemes. The
author names a number of public collections in Northern Italy (in Ravenna, Bologna,
Cremona) which have similar works. All three paintings are of the Virgin and Child;
in two of them the Virgin is of the type called Hodighitria, while in the third she is
shown as Galaktotrophousa. The author dates the works, which are reproduced at the
end of the article, to the sixteenth and seventeenth centuries.

Publishing and the Media

Books and the book trade

226 **Catalogo dei libri in commercio.** (Catalogue of books in print.)
     Milano: Editrice Bibliografica, 1975- . annual.

Includes works published in San Marino. It is in three volumes arranged by subject, author and title, with a list of publishers in the author and subject volumes.

227 **Produzione tipografica ed attività editoriale nella Repubblica di
     San Marino dal XVII secolo ai nostri giorni.** (Printing and
     publishing in the Republic of San Marino from the seventeenth century
     to the present day.)
     Elisabetta Righi Iwanejko.   In: *Biblioteca e Ricerca.*   San Marino:
     AIEP, 1983, p. 63-95. (Quaderni del Dicastero Pubblica Istruzione e
     Cultura, no. 2).

Printing came late to San Marino. The author of this article, the current director of the State Library, explains that initally this was because the population was small enough to be able to communicate effectively by word of mouth. Later it was the government that was unwilling to allow printing, and it was not until the political crisis in Italy had ended in the unification of the country that Giuseppe Angeli, a local schoolmaster, was able to set up San Marino's first workshop in 1879. The article contains a large number of bibliographical references, and is followed by a selection of photographs of key nineteenth- and twentieth-century printers.

Periodicals

228   **Periodici e organi d'informazione.** (Periodicals and information
       publications.)
       In: *Guida Titano: annuario amministrativo ed economico della
       Repubblica di San Marino. 1994-1995.*   San Marino: Edizioni del
       Titano, 1994, section 200.
These pages list periodicals currently published in San Marino. For each entry, a
contact address is given, together with the year in which the periodical was founded,
the number of copies produced and the means of distribution.

Newspapers

229   **Corriere di San Marino.** (San Marino Courier.)
       Borgo Maggiore, San Marino : Bruschi Edizioni, 1993- . daily.
Daily newspaper covering news, politics, entertainment and sport.

230   **Il Quotidiano Sammarinese**. (The San Marino daily newspaper.)
       Murata, San Marino: Società Editoriale Il Quotidiano Sammarinese,
       1993- . daily.
Daily newspaper covering news, politics, culture, sport and entertainment.

Directories

231 Current European directories.
Compiled and edited by Terri O'Connor. Beckenham, England: CBD Research, 1994. 3rd ed. 1 vol.

The section on San Marino is on pages 281-2, giving details of Kompass Italia (a company information directory which contains entries for 54,000 businesses in Italy and San Marino), and the San Marino Telephone Directory (Numbers for San Marino appear in Italy's Forlì region directories (see item no. 232).

232 Forlì e provincia, Repubblica di San Marino: elenco ufficiale degli abbonati al telefono. (Forlì and its province, Republic of San Marino: official directory of telephone subscribers.)
Società Italiana per l'Esercizio delle Telecomunicazioni. Turin, Italy: SIP. annual. 1 vol.

Telephones and related services in San Marino are provided by the Italian state telecommunications company SIP (Società Italiana per l'Esercizio delle Telecomunicazioni). The Republic is too small to merit its own directory and is included at the end of the local directory for Forlì and Rimini. The section begins with a list of all government and other official numbers, and is followed by an A–Z sequence that incorporates both private and business subscribers. There are no separate 'yellow pages' for this area.

233 Guida Titano: annuario amministrativo ed economico della Repubblica di San Marino. (Guida Titano: administrative and economic annual to the Republic of San Marino.)
San Marino: Edizioni del Titano, 1994. 1 vol.

This is probably the most comprehensive guide to the country's public bodies, associations, commercial companies and press, containing around 300 pages. The work is largely a list of names and contacts arranged by subject, but some sections also give introductory paragraphs. The text is principally in Italian, but all headings and selected other material have been translated into English. The guide is well indexed.

234 **The international directory of government.**

London: Europa Publications, 1990. 697p.

San Marino's government ministers and their departments are listed in the section dedicated to the Republic (p. 500-1). Some information about banks and judiciary bodies is also given.

235 **Kompass: annuario generale dell'economia italiana.** (Kompass: general yearbook of the Italian economy.)

Turin, Italy: Kompass Italia. annual. 3 vols.

Italy in this annual survey includes San Marino. The first two volumes are arranged according to class of commodity, with Sanmarinese products being interfiled with those made by Italian companies. Volume three is arranged geographically. There is a three-page section on San Marino in the 1994 edition (p. 2551-3) giving company names, addresses and contact numbers as well as details about the workforce, banking arrangements, products and exports. The work contains English and German translations.

236 **Museums of the world.**

Munich, Germany; New York; London: K. G. Saur, 1992. 622p.

(Handbooks of International Documentation and Information, no. 16).

The section on San Marino lists five museums, giving their addresses and subject coverage.

237 **The world directory of diplomatic representation.**

London: Europa Publications, 1992. 671p.

This work gives listings of names, job titles, addresses and telephone/facsimile numbers for ambassadors, consuls and other diplomatic staff around the world. The section on San Marino (p. 302) lists foreign representatives in the Republic. Sections on other countries give details of Sanmarinese diplomats abroad.

238 **World directory of parliaments.**

Geneva: Inter-Parliamentary Union, 1979- . annual. 1 vol.

This annual directory gives details in English and French about the Great and General Council in the section on San Marino, including number of members, terms of office, election dates and contact addresses and telephone numbers.

239 **The world of learning.**

London: Europa, 1949- . annual. 1 vol.

This directory of learned societies, libraries, museums, institutes of higher education and universities contains a one-page entry for San Marino, with up-to-date addresses and telephone numbers.

240 **Yearbook of international organizations.**

Edited by the Union of International Associations. Munich, Germany: K. G. Saur, 1983- . annual. 3 vols.

Volume two, the 'Geographic volume', of international organization participation, contains a section on San Marino, giving details of secretariats and membership lists.

Bibliographies

241 **Bibliografia delle fonti sulla costituzione di movimenti, associazioni, partiti politici e su aspetti della questione sociale della Repubblica di San Marino tra il 1860 e il 1924: i materiali della Biblioteca di Stato.** (Bibliography of sources on the establishment of movements, associations and political parties, and of social issues in the Republic of San Marino from 1860 to 1924: the collections of the State Library.)
Pier Paolo Guardigli. In: *Biblioteca e Ricerca.* San Marino: AIEP, 1983, p. 139-68. (Quaderni del Dicastero Pubblica Istruzione e Cultura, no. 2).
This bibliography of socio-political material contains items printed between 1860 and 1924, and is based on the collections of the State Library. There are three listings. The first is of books and pamphlets published from 1876 to 1923, and is arranged by subject. The second contains manifestos and other leaflets printed between 1877 and 1922, and is arranged chronologically. Finally, there is an alphabetical listing of periodicals published from 1881 to 1923. There are no annotations.

242 **Bibliografia delle tradizioni popolari di San Marino.** (Bibliography of popular traditions in San Marino.)
Giovanni Crocioni. San Marino: Filippo della Balda, 1947. 93p.
Crocioni's is a short bibliography of works deals with social and cultural customs and traditions relating to San Marino. It contains an essay on the historical toponymy of the country, and another on poetry in the local dialect.

243 **Bibliografia sammarinese.** (San Marino bibliography.)
Maria Antonietta Bonelli. San Marino: Dicastero alla Pubblica Istruzione e Cultura, 1985- .
Using the works of Carlo Padiglione (Naples, 1872) and Luigi de Montalbo (Paris, 1898) as a basis, this bibliography on San Marino is sponsored by the State and is

intended to be a definitive work of around twenty volumes, three of which have been published to date. Its scope is wide: works wholly or partly about San Marino, all works by Sanmarinese writers, all works printed within the country's borders, Sanmarinese newspaper articles of an historical or literary nature, and significant works on events and people that have had a significant influence on the Republic's history (Cardinal Alberoni, Giuseppe Garibaldi, and so on). The material is arranged alphabetically by author, but with a list of items without personal authors at the end of each letter arranged by title. Entries are annotated and often include short extracts. Each volume contains indexes of people, places and subjects.

244   **Cento anni di studi sulla Romagna, 1861-1961: bibliografia storica.**
      (One hundred years of studies on Romagna, 1861-1961: an historical
      bibliography.)
      Augusto Vasina.   Faenza, Italy: Fratelli Lega, 1962-63. 3 vols.
      (Collana di Saggi e Repertori della Società di Studi Romagnoli, no. 7).
This three-volume bibliography covers the cultural area of Romagna, with an emphasis on its history. The general material in Volume one may be of interest to the scholar of San Marino, but there is a lengthy section devoted entirely to the Republic in Volume two (p. 493-533). The entries are arranged by period and virtually all the works referred to are in Italian.

245   **Dizionario bibliografico e istorico della Repubblica di S. Marino.**
      (Bibliographical and historical dictionary of the Republic of San
      Marino.)
      Carlo Padiglione.   Naples, Italy: Tipografia della Gazzetta di Napoli,
      1872. 491p.
This detailed bibliography contains a wide range of material published principally during the eighteenth and nineteenth centuries. Its strength lies in its inclusion of a significant number of ephemera and references to chapters and pages in works dealing with broader subject areas. The volume is arranged by author, with an index of names at the end. Each entry is annotated.

246   **Dizionario bibliografico iconografico della Repubblica di San
      Marino.** (Bibliographical-iconographic dictionary of the Republic of
      San Marino.)
      Luigi de Montalbo.   Paris: The author, 1898. 321p. map.
A privately produced bibliography based largely on the Baron de Montalbo's library. It contains references to works in various languages, arranged alphabetically by author or title. There are many illustrations, mainly portraits, and the work is well indexed. An appendix lists important manuscripts, and there is a chapter on heraldry in which the shields of the Republic's principal families are depicted.

Indexes

There follow three separate indexes: authors (personal and corporate); titles; and subjects. Title entries are italicized and refer either to the main titles, or to other works cited in the annotations. The numbers refer to bibliographical entry rather than page numbers. Individual index entries are arranged in alphabetical sequence.

Index of Authors

Sozzi, G. P. 110, 116, 130
Spadolini, G. 101
Suzzi Valli, A. 32, 35-6

T

Tagliavini, C. 81
Tassi, F. 30
Turchini, A. 85

U

Union of International Associations 240
University of Bologna 192

V

Valli, M. 219
Vasina, A. 244

W

Waagenaar, S. 4
Wasserman, S. R. 154

Z

Zàngheri, P. 34
Zani, G. 60, 183, 187
Zocca, E. 20
Zucconi, G. 189
Zuppetta (Professor) 125

Index of Titles

Index of Subjects

97

Map of San Marino

This map shows the location of the towns and villages.

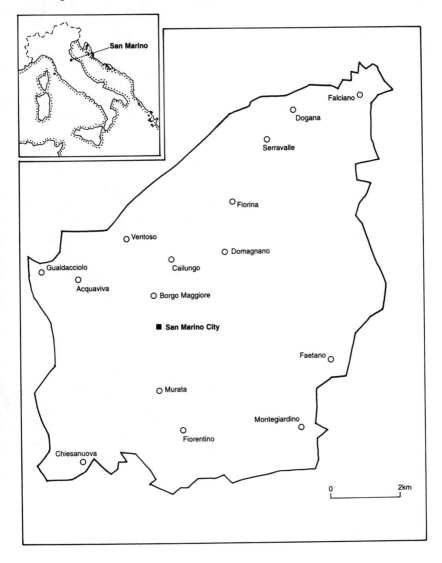

ALSO FROM CLIO PRESS

INTERNATIONAL ORGANIZATIONS SERIES

Each volume in the International Organizations Series is either devoted to one specific organization, or to a number of different organizations operating in a particular region, or engaged in a specific field of activity. The scope of the series is wide-ranging and includes intergovernmental organizations, international non-governmental organizations, and national bodies dealing with international issues. The series is aimed mainly at the English-speaker and each volume provides a selective, annotated, critical bibliography of the organization, or organizations, concerned. The bibliographies cover books, articles, pamphlets, directories, databases and theses and, wherever possible, attention is focused on material about the organizations rather than on the organizations' own publications. Notwithstanding this, the most important official publications, and guides to those publications, will be included. The views expressed in individual volumes, however, are not necessarily those of the publishers.

VOLUMES IN THE SERIES